Dwig

FRIESEN

The
Connect
Effect

The
Connect
Effect

BUILDING STRONG PERSONAL, PROFESSIONAL, AND VIRTUAL NETWORKS

Michael Dulworth

BERRETT-KOEHLER PUBLISHERS, INC.
San Francisco

Berrett-Koehler Publishers, Inc.
235 Montgomery Street, Suite 650
San Francisco, CA 94104-2916
Tel: (415) 288-0260   Fax: (415) 362-2512   www.bkconnection.com

Ordering Information
Quantity sales. Special discounts are available on quantity purchases by corporations, associations, and others. For details, contact the "Special Sales Department" at the Berrett-Koehler address above.
Individual sales. Berrett-Koehler publications are available through most bookstores. They can also be ordered directly from Berrett-Koehler: Tel: (800) 929-2929; Fax: (802) 864-7626; www.bkconnection.com
Orders for college textbook/course adoption use. Please contact Berrett-Koehler: Tel: (800) 929-2929; Fax: (802) 864-7626.
Orders by U.S. trade bookstores and wholesalers. Please contact Ingram Publisher Services, Tel: (800) 509-4887; Fax: (800) 838-1149; E-mail: customer.service@ingrampublisher services.com; or visit www.ingrampublisherservices.com/Ordering for details about electronic ordering.

Berrett-Koehler and the BK logo are registered trademarks of Berrett-Koehler Publishers, Inc.

Printed in the United States of America

Berrett-Koehler books are printed on long-lasting acid-free paper. When it is available, we choose paper that has been manufactured by environmentally responsible processes. These may include using trees grown in sustainable forests, incorporating recycled paper, minimizing chlorine in bleaching, or recycling the energy produced at the paper mill.

Library of Congress Cataloging-in-Publication Data
Dulworth, Mike, 1962-
  The connect effect : building strong personal, professional, and virtual networks / Michael Dulworth.
    p. cm.
  Includes bibliographical references and index.
  ISBN 978-1-57675-462-7 (hardcover : alk. paper)
  1. Social networks. 2. Business networks. I. Title.
HM741.D84   2008
650.1'3—dc22   2007039226

FIRST EDITION
13 12 11 10 09 08   10 9 8 7 6 5 4 3 2 1

Cover design by ALIAN Design.
Interior Design and composition by Beverly Butterfield, Girl of the West Productions.
Copyediting by PeopleSpeak.
Indexing by Rachel Rice.

To my parents,
the first members of my network

Contents

Preface

Networks can change the world;
every node matters.
ANONYMOUS

Everybody knows what networking is. People network at a luncheon or conference by exchanging business cards, telling each other about their jobs. But it can be much more than that. When done effectively, networking is about more than the number of business cards you hand out, the size of your Rolodex, or the numbers stored in your BlackBerry: it can be a way of life if you want to take it that far. It's about how you see yourself and how you connect with the world around you. When you make networking a priority, you can put what I call the "Connect Effect" to work for you.

I define the Connect Effect as the positive outcome derived from investing in your network. The benefits of the Connect Effect are many and varied. As you connect personally with more and more carefully chosen people, you increase your ability to advance your career, enhance your personal life, and accomplish things you may have thought were impossible. In this book, I'm going to show you the multiple benefits of strong, dynamic networks and the best ways to grow and enhance them.

Strong networks involve more than just widening the circle of people you know. They foster deeper learning and broader exposure to a variety of issues—as you will discover. An effective network can make you more knowledgeable and better grounded, as well as a more agile learner and a better collaborator. When you become a skilled networker, you can address challenges and make the most of opportunities at the fast pace essential for success in today's world.

But networks are not just about getting ahead; they can help you make a big difference on the issues you are passionate about. Networks can even change the world. Look at just a few ways networks are making an impact:

- ► The Linux computer operating system was largely developed on a volunteer basis by a network of users and developers and is used today throughout the world on desktop computers, servers, and even supercomputers.

- ► President Clinton's Global Initiative brings together a community of global leaders to devise and implement innovative solutions to some of the world's most pressing challenges, including poverty, climate change, global health, and religious and ethnic conflicts.

- ► Procter & Gamble's Connect + Develop program uses an open network of thousands of scientists to solve problems that P&G needs to overcome. The goal of C plus D is to look outside P&G's corporate walls to find new products, technology, packaging, design, processes, and business models. P&G is also a member of the InnoCentive network, where "Seekers" post their tough R&D challenges on the confidential InnoCentive Web site. More than eighteen thousand leading scientists and researchers in 125 countries around the world can then submit solutions to scientific challenges and receive a financial award for delivering the best solutions.

- ► Grameen Bank's founder, Muhammad Yunus, formed a cooperative to provide microloans to "solidarity groups" of poor women in Bangladesh and won the 2006 Nobel Peace

Prize for "efforts to create economic and social development from below."[1]

At their heart, these initiatives are all networks. People meet people; share their interests, passions, and knowledge; help one another; and form binding relationships and associations that often result in great accomplishments. This is how human beings work—at our core we're social animals.

Few of us are born successful networkers, however, and networking is a skill that's rarely taught. To accelerate your personal and professional growth, you need to make the active development and enhancement of your networks a priority in your life. I wrote this book to provide you with a simple networking framework (the right people, the right conversations, the right time) and set of tools for developing your personal, professional, and online networks. *The Connect Effect* is about leveraging networks to enhance success—success in one's personal life, success on the job, success in one's career, and success in a broader social context, improving the world in some way.

As I will explain later in this book, most of the success I have achieved in life as an entrepreneur, published author, business owner, and more, I owe to networking. There is almost nothing that I can't do or accomplish—or do better, more efficiently, and more effectively—through my network. So when I decided to write this book, it was only natural for me to explore my network and do more networking to help me gather the insights of many.

I ended up connecting with more than thirty people from all walks of life in the course of working on this book. I searched out experts on networking (people who study it) and expert networkers (people who have built extraordinary networks). As you read this book, you will meet and get to know many members of my network as they share their networking insights with you.

You will learn from people who have studied networking for many years, such as Rob Cross of the University of Virginia, coauthor of *The Hidden Power of Social Networks*, and Richard Leider, a leading executive coach and bestselling author of *Repacking Your Bags*. And we will also explore the insights of some very successful networkers, such as Barbara Howes, vice president, Disney University, the Walt Disney Company; John Foster, head of talent management and organization development at IDEO, the cutting-edge design firm; and Marshall Goldsmith, the bestselling author and leadership coach.

What's Ahead

The Connect Effect is for all who want to have a more rewarding life—personally and professionally—no matter what they are focused on or what goals they have set for themselves, from entry-level employees to senior executives, from entrepreneurs just starting out to seasoned business owners. The book is divided into two parts. The first part offers guidelines on becoming a more effective networker. As you will discover, you can do a few simple things that will boost your networking skills tremendously—and if you want to get more involved in networking, you will learn how it can change your life.

The introduction, "The Power of Networks," explains all the many benefits networks offer. You will discover that networking is about much more than opening doors and advancing your career.

Chapter 1, "What's Your Networking Quotient?" will help you assess your current ability to network—your networking quotient, or NQ—and explain how you can map out how extensive and solid your existing network is.

Networking doesn't have to be complicated, but it does have to be consistent. Chapter 2, "Network Early, Network Often," draws on my and others' experience to explain the basics of networking and the importance of making it a habitual part of your daily activities. Chapter 3, "Building Your Network," explains how to use key tools, such as the network accelerator, to systematically expand and strengthen your network.

In chapter 4, "What's Your Personal Brand?" I explain how developing a consistent and authentic personal image or brand can make your networking much more effective. If businesses are supported and sustained by a wise, experienced board of directors, then why shouldn't this work for individuals—you, for example? Chapter 5, "Entering the Network Zone," shows how it can.

The second part of the book shows how to harness the power of specific types of networking. Chapter 6, "Networking Peer-to-Peer," explains how to create and use a network of peers who have job roles and responsibilities similar to your own. Have a specific problem at work? Similar problems have probably been dealt with successfully by others who can share their experience with you. Every organization has an organizational chart showing lines of authority. But alongside these official lines of authority are usually invisible networks that actually account for much of the decision making. In chapter 7, "Tapping Organizational Networks," I explain how to ferret out these networks and put them to use for you.

A community of practice is a group of people who join together to help each other solve problems and develop expertise in an area of shared interest. Unlike a peer network, it brings together people from a multitude of disciplines. Chapter 8, "Joining Communities of Practice," offers insight into the power of these more formal networks. Web sites like MySpace and Facebook have hundreds of millions of users all over the world who make connections online. Chapter 9, "Virtual Networking," offers a quick overview of online networking and offers some dos and don'ts for networking in virtual space. The conclusion, "The Future of Networking," explores some of the issues we will be facing in the years ahead.

As you read what follows, my sincere wish is that you will find the journey interesting and enlightening. Networking can open up exciting opportunities, but as we will discover, the best networkers know that networking is really about helping others first. Tim Sanders, chief solutions officer at Yahoo!, puts it this way: "All of your knowledge won't amount to much if you don't have a network of people to share it with and enough compassion for the people in that network to understand that your success is a direct result of their success."[2]

Networking is something that we all do naturally every day, though we may call it by different names. One of the purposes of this book is to help you to see that you already have a personal network and are already enjoying the Connect Effect. Once you are aware, you can then begin to employ the skills contained here to bring you even more benefits—and maybe even change the world for the benefit of others.

Introduction

The Power of Networks

The first time I saw the power of the Connect Effect was when I was trying to get into college. I didn't study very hard in high school, and this was reflected in my B-minus average. So I asked my uncle Dick for help. He had attended the University of Michigan and still lived close to the school in Ann Arbor, Michigan. He and Aunt Anita knew many professors and administrators at the university. Because of their connections, I got an interview with an admissions officer and was able to talk my way into summer school. The admissions officer wasn't willing to overlook my lackluster grades, but he did make a deal with me: if I proved myself in summer school, the university would admit me in the fall as a freshman. I did and it did.

The benefits of the Connect Effect can be as varied and rich as we make them. Consider some of these comments from the real-life people I talked to (through networking!) as I researched this book:

- "Networking feeds my soul . . . It stimulates my thinking and takes me to different possibilities."

- "I can't think of much that I've achieved in either life or career without networking: it's the currency for getting things done."

- "Networking pulls me in all kinds of unintended directions, often leading to being in the right place at the right time with the right people."

- "Networking has totally changed my life and career. Everything I do is through a network."

- "Networking is the means by which I've landed all of my jobs in my adult life."

- "Leadership is a collaborative effort. And it takes a network of people."

- "It takes a network of people to realize a dream."

Think about those comments for a moment. Networking can change your life, feed your soul, and help you realize your dreams. Who wouldn't want to network and achieve the power of the Connect Effect?

As your network of friends and associates grows and improves, this Connect Effect increases rapidly. In fact, the Connect Effect is exponential in nature, not linear, because each new connection brings his or her own network. The Connect Effect truly proves that $1 + 1 = 4$ (or more)!

Throughout the book, I'll provide personal stories, frameworks, tools, and resources to help you become a better networker so that you, in turn, can be happier and more successful. I draw from my experience in building, nurturing, and leveraging my personal network, as well as over twenty-five years of experience in helping people develop their own, and on the insights and wisdom of expert networkers, network researchers, and people who have professional responsibility to manage networks. I have facilitated all types of networks throughout my career. Today, I am the CEO of a professional networking company. In many ways, networking is my life, and I embrace its potential both personally and professionally. We'll begin by looking at some of the many Connect Effects networks can bring.

The Uses of Networks

Let's look more carefully at exactly how networks can be used to achieve personal and professional success—to realize our dreams. In my own life, and in discussions with others, I have identified a number of critical areas in which networks can enhance our lives:

- Personal satisfaction
- Career guidance
- Door opening
- Problem solving and feedback
- Learning and expertise
- Changing the world

I have firsthand experience with each of these Connect Effects of networking. What's more, my research on networking and conversations with others show exactly how powerful networks are in each of these areas. Let's take a look.

Personal Satisfaction

On the most basic level, networking can bring deep personal satisfaction. We are, after all, social animals. Making friends, helping others, collaborating on a worthwhile project are all very satisfying experiences that can feed your soul, as Nisha Advani, director of executive development at Genentech told me. Born and raised in India, Nisha has lived on three continents and now focuses on using science principles to enhance leadership and organizational effectiveness at Genentech. She sees networking as deeply satisfying: "Networking feeds my soul. It helps me to stay alert and continuously learn, and those are very deep values for me. I appreciate having a network that brings up a lot of rich ideas, both personally, in my social space and family, as well as professionally. It stimulates my thinking and takes me to different possibilities."

The person in my life who best embodies the personal satisfaction inherent in networking is my aunt Norma. At age eighty-nine, she makes new friends every time she leaves the house, just for the sheer fun of it. My cousin Kristan describes breakfast at a local café with Aunt Norma (Kristan's grandma):

> She greeted everyone we passed, and while we waited for a table, she struck up a conversation with a mother and her twentysomething daughter who seemed somewhat distressed. Grandma talked comfortably with them as if she had known them her whole life. They shared their sadness that the daughter, who was pregnant, her husband, and their little girl were moving to Germany the following day.
>
> Grandma listened, smiled, and in a very positive and matter-of-fact voice said to the mother, "Well, you're just going to have to get yourself over to Germany to visit!" They all laughed and agreed. As an observer, I could see the tension in their faces melt away—the result of a random and brief encounter with a woman who, in her almost nine decades on the planet, has never left North America.

On Norma's eighty-eighth birthday, she told me about the numerous phone calls and the sixty birthday cards she had received. "And those are only the friends that are still alive," she said.

I encourage you to think of someone in your own life who creates networks of caring people simply through having a friendly and loving manner. You may come up with several such people.

Career Guidance

In 1983, I graduated from the University of Michigan with a degree in history. At that point, I dipped into my rather limited network—specifically, my dad and my uncle Jack—for help finding a job.

My uncle Jack was well connected from his work as an insurance broker in Houston, Texas, and was able to set up interviews with the offices of James Baker III, chief of staff in the Reagan White House, and Texas senator Lloyd Benson. Through his own networks, my dad arranged for an interview with the U.S. Department of Labor. I received job offers from all three places but chose the job at the Department of Labor because it paid the most ($10,300 per year!).

This was my first big lesson in the power of the Connect Effect: three great job offers for a young man straight out of college and all of them due to the robust networks developed by my father and uncle. Of course, many others have similar stories. One of the people I interviewed for this book is Jory Des Jardins, a smart, humorous, Web-savvy entrepreneur, writer, and blogger. Jory coined the phrase "networking: it's the currency for getting things done," which I quoted above. Jory makes the point that people starting out need advocates in today's fast-paced, competitive job market:

After graduating from college, I sent out résumés, cold-called for jobs, did what anyone without contacts would do, and nothing ever came of it. I'd hoped that my grade point average would be all that I needed, but I learned early on that my accomplishments wouldn't help me unless I had the right advocates. Fortunately, a friend's father put in a good word for me with a publishing house, and I got my first "real" job. I didn't know it at the time, but that was networking. From there everything I had, from jobs to a wedding caterer, I got through networking. Still, I don't think I appreciated the powerful impact that networking had on getting things done until I cofounded BlogHer. I met my partners through networking, and then we tapped a network of influential women bloggers to help us build our first conference in four months. We never would have been able to tap into pockets of smaller blogging communities nor get the word out about our event—which sold out—so quickly without a network. The entire process of building a community, and later a company, was the result of tapping a few key people, who in turn tapped their respective communities, who tapped thousands through their blogs.

Most people appreciate how networking can help in finding and landing jobs. But many don't understand that it's actually *the most important thing* you can do in your job search. Think about it: the bestselling bible for job hunters, *What Color Is Your Parachute?* is essentially a guide to networking.

Door Opening

Closely related to career guidance, "door opening" refers to the introductions people in your network can make for you, whether you are in the job market or not. Networking opens doors for you that would otherwise remain shut; it gives you access to people.

To illustrate the power a network has to open doors, let me describe how I got a book published at John Wiley & Sons. These days, it's very difficult to get published as a first-time author unless you're a recognized expert in your field. But my network came through.

I'd been renovating houses as a hobby since I was about thirty years old. I renovated a condo in Washington, DC, a historic farmhouse in West Virginia, and, with my wife, a house in Sonoma, California. While renovating the house in Sonoma, I got the idea to write a book on the strategy and execution of renovating houses to build personal wealth, since I'd made quite a bit of money on my first two renovations. I put together a one-page outline of the book and e-mailed it to a contact I had at Wiley, Larry Alexander. (I had met Larry earlier, when he was with Jossey-Bass Publishers, through an old University of Michigan connection, Dan Denison, whom I'd met when he was a professor at the University. Dan was working with another professor at the University, Robert Quinn, who had published a number of books at Jossey-Bass.) The next day, Larry put me in touch with the head of Wiley's real estate publishing group, and within two weeks I had a contract and an advance to write the book, which I wrote with my wife (*Renovate to Riches*, Dulworth and Goodwin, John Wiley & Sons, 2003).

John Foster, head of talent management and organization development at IDEO, a well-known design company, says he is "the living stereotype" of the connected networker. He told me that networking opens all sorts of doors for him and gave me an example: "Very recently I got involved in a corporate roundtable that's sponsored by Harvard University. Through my participation, I've received many excellent references and connections. It even led to my former university asking me to be on an advisory board for one of their colleges."

Joanne Black, the author of *No More Cold Calling*, offered me a different perspective on the value of getting introductions and referrals from people in your network. When you are introduced by a mutual acquaintance, she pointed out, not only is the door opened, but things are different when you walk through it: "When we get a qualified referral, which means someone wants to talk to us, we're presold. We have a different kind of conversation. We have credibility. We have trust."

The ability to use networks to open doors, gain introductions to people, and gain access is important for virtually anything you need to do in your personal and professional life.

Problem Solving

Networks are a powerful problem-solving resource that people naturally turn to when they need help. Recently a business contact called me and said his daughter had injured herself while sailing and needed to see a specialist in San Francisco immediately. She had just moved to the area and didn't know where to go. One of my company's board members had recently been injured in a skiing accident, so I asked her for help. She gave me the name of the best orthopedic surgeon in the Bay Area, and the next day my colleague's daughter had an appointment and the best medical care.

Another business colleague told me that he was having trouble finding a publisher for a book he and his business partners were writing. I sent an introductory e-mail to Cedric Crocker at Jossey-Bass Publishers, and within a few months my colleague had a book contract.

Rob Cross, whom we will visit several times over the course of this book, says people often don't realize how top performers solve problems. Rob is a professor in the management department of the University of Virginia's McIntire School of Commerce and coauthor of *The Hidden Power of Social Networks*. He is also the founder of the Network Roundtable, a group of forty organizations that research networks and apply network techniques to critical business issues. He generously offered to spend time with me explaining his research on networks.

"I became interested in networks about ten years ago when I was working for Arthur Anderson," Rob told me. "At that time, I was really focused on improving knowledge-worker productivity." "Knowledge worker" is a term that was originally popularized by the management guru Peter Drucker and refers to people whose jobs primarily involve creating, managing, or disseminating information. Rob told me that when he first looked into how to improve the productivity of knowledge workers, everybody at that time was treating it as a computer database issue. "Yet when I talked to people about how they solved problems, nobody ever said, 'I jump on the knowledge repository or a database.' Instead, they reached out to their network when they had a new client, a new project, or some sort of problem they were trying to resolve. They said, 'We pick up the phone, walk down the hall, and work our network in various ways to get information, resources, or approvals or other things we need to get something done.'"

When you have a network of thoughtful, experienced, and smart people, you actually have a cadre of "consultants" you can call on to help you deal with difficult personal and professional issues. These are people who have often faced similar problems, opportunities, and challenges. There is significant comfort in knowing that you have a group of trusted and objective colleagues you can call on when you need help, advice, and support.

Two kinds of networks are especially effective in problem solving: peer-to-peer networks and communities of practice. A peer-to-peer network encompasses people who have similar roles and responsibilities and face similar problems. A community of practice is a group of people who join together to help each other solve problems and develop expertise in an area of shared interest. We will explore peer-to-peer networks in depth in chapter 6 and communities of practice in much more detail in chapter 8.

Learning and Expertise

When we think about learning, we tend to focus on the obvious sources of instruction: courses, books, self-study, and the like. In my own experience, which is corroborated by others, networking can be a more powerful resource for learning than any of these.

I recently did a Google search on the phrase "learning network" and got more than a million hits. Learning is a prime Connect Effect. Talk to people who make it a habit to reach out and network, and you'll hear time and again how much they learn from others. On a personal level, we learn about good books, new movies, and great restaurants from people in our networks. On a professional level, we learn about new developments in our fields, what's happening in other fields, who is breaking new ground, who can help us learn new skills, and much, much more.

Early in my career, my dad set up meetings with five very accomplished people so I could discuss my career goals and aspirations with them. I met with Brian Usilaner, who worked for the Office of Management and Budget and the U.S. General Accounting Office (GAO); Tom Schneider, a prominent labor lawyer; Malcolm Lovell, a former undersecretary of labor and fellow at the Brookings Institution; Bill Hunt, vice president of human resources at SkyChef; and Michael Maccoby, management guru and author of *The Gamesman*. I asked each of these prominent men to tell me about his career and career progression as well as what had led to his success. I also discussed my own career, my career interests, and whether I should go to graduate school, then listened intently to their advice and guidance. I learned so much from these meetings, talking to people face-to-face. They had more impact than reading a slew of books could ever achieve.

Bill Morin, the founder and former chairman of Drake Beam Morin, the well-known career management firm, told me that networking is "a vital force for learning about where you want to go with your career, learning about what you need to know about your profession." Bill got into my network through my father's. (My dad hired Bill out of graduate school and they've stayed friends ever since.)

Learning from your network can be more powerful than other types of learning because you are often learning from other people who have "been there and done that." Etienne Wenger, author of *Cultivating Communities of Practice*, is a leading authority on communities of practice who is working with my company to develop a proprietary community operating philosophy and framework. He explained to me one reason why networks are such powerful resources for learning:

> I think that there is a shift happening in the world today where people are starting to recognize that in fact network interactions are one of the keys to learning not only for professionals but for people in general. Because when you have a peer network you hear the story of someone else who is in a similar situation to you so there is almost an immediate validity to what you are hearing because you recognize that this person faces the same problems. There is something about hearing the words of someone who is a peer that makes the relevance of the knowledge that you get very immediate.

Networks are often set up for the explicit goal of learning. My friend Marshall Goldsmith, a leading executive coach and author of the bestselling book *What Got You Here Won't Get You There*, formed the Learning Network about ten years ago. He invited other executive coaches, executive development professionals, and leadership experts to come together to share experiences and learn from each other at annual meetings. He asked people such as Sally Helgesen (author of *The Female Advantage*) and Jim Kouzes (coauthor of *The Leadership Challenge*) to join. Jim told me, "Marshall invited me to join that network. Marshall Goldsmith was somebody I was working with because of a publication he was working on. I recently attended the tenth meeting of the Learning Network. It's a very

informal meeting. There's an agenda, but it's not always followed. We get together. We share experiences." And everyone,
he said, learns a lot from one another.

Innovation cannot happen without learning. They go hand
in hand, as John Zapolski, a partner with the Management Innovation Group, told me when I interviewed him. A former
filmmaker, technologist, and designer who has worked at
Wells Fargo and Yahoo!, John is intensely interested in learning and innovation. According to John, networks promote
cross-fertilization, which is what innovation is all about. "I
think innovation happens most of the time by people who have
understandings from one domain and are able to take lessons
from that domain and apply them to a whole separate domain—
maybe taking a business model from the financial services industry and applying that to the airline industry. That's a very
ripe source of innovation. And that only happens when there
are connections that allow people to cross-fertilize like that."

He added that it is important to focus beyond your own
area of specialization: "Industries, domains, and functions tend
to get very insular if left to their own natural tendencies. Actively seeking to be in touch with people who are outside of an
industry or domain that you belong to is a vital component to
being able to bring in new thinking that ultimately is going
to drive innovation."

A rich, rewarding life is very much dependent on continu-
ous learning, and networking is an important learning tool.

Changing the World

During the past year, in the blocks surrounding my office in
downtown San Francisco, I noticed a number of middle-aged
women sitting on the sidewalk with begging cups. By engaging
one of these women in conversation, I learned that she and
most of the others were between the ages of fifty and sixty-five.

Women over sixty-five are able to use Social Security payments to pay for lodging, but those without Social Security or other means of support often become destitute and homeless. Most avoid homeless shelters because they have suffered abuse from homeless men in the shelters.

At present, I am engaged in what I call the "VeraMax Project" (named after my two grandmothers, Vera Dulworth and Maxine Cross). Because of someone in my network, I attended a Democratic fund-raiser in the fall of 2006, where I met the mayor of San Francisco, Gavin Newsom, who introduced me to the most senior official in his administration focused on homeless issues, Trent Rhorer. Trent then set up a meeting between the team I put together to bring the VeraMax House to reality (a lawyer, an architect, a clinical psychologist, a commercial builder, an interior designer, etc.) and the heads of the key agencies in San Francisco that deal with the homeless issue. I'm confident that through the Connect Effect, this project will ultimately result in a shelter for these women, enabling them to leave the streets and start new lives.

This example is just one illustration of how strong networks can change the world. Other, more far-reaching examples include President Clinton's Global Initiative and Muhammad Yunus, winner of the 2006 Nobel Peace Prize, who formed a cooperative to provide microloans to poor women in Bangladesh. (I discussed both of these in the preface.) These are networks designed not to help their participants but to change the world. Remember this quotation from Margaret Mead: "Never doubt that a small group of thoughtful, committed citizens can change the world. Indeed, it is the only thing that ever has."

Mutual Success and the Connect Effect

It's important to emphasize that the benefits discussed here need to be mutual. As a skilled networker, your need is to see that all the people in your network achieve success. The old adage "You get what you give" is doubly true with networks. Just as you can use your network to open doors, you should open doors for others. Just as you turn to people in your network to deal with problems you encounter, you should make sure you are generous in your offers to help others deal with the challenges they face. And as you seek to learn from others, you should help others learn and share your knowledge and experience freely.

One of the first keys to success is to extend yourself and help the people in your network, regardless of whether you think the favor will be returned. Marshall Goldsmith expressed this idea very directly when we talked: "To me, a key to networking is not focusing on what you can get—the key to networking is focusing on what you can give. My general philosophy is very simple. Find great people, give them things, and work on a relationship where they try to give me as much as I give them."

Virtually everyone I talked to for this book agreed with this philosophy. And they all readily agreed to spend time with me to share their insights, knowledge, and experience. They were eager to give to you, the reader of this book, what help they could, never having met you. That's what people who truly see networking as a way of life are all about.

The more goodwill you spread across your network, the more powerful your network will be. And the more powerful your network is, the more profound an effect it will have on your personal and professional life.

In the next chapter, we will take a look at the status of your network right now—and see how it might be strengthened.

PART ONE

Becoming a
Highly Effective
Networker

1

What's Your Networking Quotient?

As we have seen, people are finding that strong personal, professional, and virtual networks are an increasingly essential element in their development, effectiveness, and well-being. Just look at the popularity of virtual networks such as MySpace, Flickr, LinkedIn, and Ryze. A strong network can help you navigate rapid change in a number of ways, including broadening your exposure to information and your access to expertise.

Networking is something that we all do naturally every day; we just may not call it that. The people who are most successful in life do it purposefully. This book is to help you do what you do naturally more consciously, more systematically, and more effectively.

In this chapter, you will have an opportunity to assess your NQ, or networking quotient. By having a single measure of your ability to develop strong networks—your NQ—you'll understand the strength of your network and where you can improve.

Before we get to the assessment of your NQ, let me share with you my equation for success:

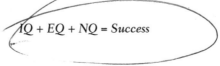

$$IQ + EQ + NQ = Success$$

IQ is the capacity to learn and understand and can be measured by standardized tests. EQ is an abbreviation for emotional intelligence quotient. In his bestselling book, *Emotional Intelligence*, Daniel Goleman asserts that EQ describes an ability, capacity, or skill to perceive, assess, and manage the emotions of oneself, of others, and of groups.

IQ is pretty much a fixed capability in all of us. You may be very smart but probably don't have the IQ of Stephen Hawking, the theoretical physicist. If we can't change our IQ and want to be more successful, what can we do?

We have some control over our EQ, so that can be a place to spend some time. It's an excellent idea for all of us to better understand ourselves and others from an emotional intelligence point of view. But this can take us only so far. We all seem to be wired in certain ways, and it's unlikely that personal understanding, psychotherapy, and self-development are going to change our innate traits or behaviors.

You probably won't be surprised, then, that I think our NQ is where we have the greatest potential for exponential change. *We have almost 100 percent control over our ability to build, nurture, and leverage our networks.* Some might argue that being an extrovert or an introvert can greatly affect, if not determine, one's NQ score, but my experience tells me that this is not the case. Some of the best networkers I've ever met are introverts—and that includes me!

So, *IQ + EQ + NQ = Success*—and the best way to improve this equation is by improving your NQ. Before you can improve it, however, you need to know what your NQ is. First, let's take a look at what makes a strong network to begin with.

The Qualities of Strong Networks

A number of years ago, Rob Cross, whom we met earlier, wrote, "What really distinguishes high performers from the rest of the pack is their ability to maintain and leverage personal networks. The most effective create and tap large, diversified networks that are rich in experience and span all organizational boundaries."[3]

Let's unpack that statement since it captures many of the qualities of strong networks.

Quantity

Size matters—you never know when an important connection will lead to a positive outcome. Virtually everyone I talked to in researching this book stressed that larger networks are better networks. John Zapolski of the Management Innovation Group, told me, "I am constantly looking to expand my network, especially people on the periphery of my network." The more people you have in your network, the more opportunities you have open to you, the more knowledge you can access, and the more talent you can tap.

Relationships

Vibrant networks are more than a collection of business cards or e-mail addresses: they are built on relationships. When you have strong relationships with people, they are more willing to spend time with you, share information with you, open doors for you, and the like. You have to build those relationships, and you do that by showing a genuine interest in other people. IDEO's John Foster told me that a critical success factor in building a strong network is "making sure that you're dealing in a reciprocal relationship. You must give back to the relationship in some meaningful way, and there has to be a real exchange of value for a network relationship to be worthwhile."

Diversity

As Rob Cross indicated, the best networks are diverse and span organizational boundaries. If everyone in your network looks like you, acts like you, and has your interests, how are you ever going to learn new things, discover new opportunities, or move in new directions? Let's hear from John Zapolski again:

> I pretty actively look for opportunities to go to new events that are really outside of the typical domain of events that I would normally go to. For example, I met a woman recently who works in innovation, but she has a deep science background, so . . . I asked her a lot of questions about her background in bioengineering and genetics and I learned a lot. Inevitably, I'll find out what groups people like this belong to or events that they go to, and maybe I'll try to attend just so I can meet people outside of my core network. I look for those new events where I can get pulled into a direction of a deeper interest.

Meeting diverse people with very different interests is the best way to keep expanding your horizons.

Quality

While quantity is important, quality is perhaps even more important. What does "quality" mean here? As Rob indicated, a network should be "rich in experience." Quality refers to people who are experienced, who have strong networks of their own, who have authority, who can open doors, and who command respect in their fields. Scott Saslow, executive director of the Institute of Executive Development, recently told me, "There is too much focus on the quantity of one's network right now (I have 8 billion colleagues from LinkedIn), and eventually the focus will shift to quality." In today's egalitarian world, we may try to treat everyone the same. But when it comes to networking, that makes little sense.

Now that we understand what makes for strong, vibrant networks, we can turn to measuring your NQ.

What's Your NQ?

Before you answer the questions below, take some time to list all the people in your network universe, which consists of three primary types of networks: (1) your personal network, (2) your professional network, and (3) your virtual network. Each plays a role in determining your NQ.

Your personal network is made up of your family, extended family, school friends and contacts, lifelong friends, and so on. It is also made up of your active friends (people you see face-to-face at least once a month) and people from your church, clubs, activities, neighborhood, and community. Your professional network includes contacts from previous jobs, colleagues from other firms, and contacts in your current organization.

Your virtual network comprises people you know only through online interactions or other non-face-to-face connections. Obviously, these networks overlap. You may be close friends with a business associate, or a family member may help you make a professional connection. And more and more networking is being done online. But these networks can serve as useful groupings in determining your NQ.

Two components go into your NQ: part A focuses on the scope and strength of your existing network, and part B focuses on how active you are in building and maintaining your network. With these components in mind, assess your NQ by honestly answering the following questions on a scale of 0–4:

Part A: Network Scope and Strength

1. How many total people are in your personal, professional, and virtual networks? Add them all together.

   0 = Under 10

   1 = 11–100

   2 = 101–200

   3 = 201–400

   4 = more than 400

2. How strong are your relationships with the people in your network? Are the people in your network just *business-card traders* (you traded cards but can hardly remember where or when), *acquaintances* (they know who you are and will probably return a call), *personal contacts* (they'll do a favor if you ask), or *close friends* (you can count on them when the chips are down)?

   0 = All business

   1 = Mostly acquaintances

   2 = Lots of personal contacts

   3 = A mix of personal contacts and close friends

   4 = Mostly close friends with a few personal contacts and
       acquaintances

3. How diverse is your network? If everyone you know is the same age and sex as you, shares your cultural background, and works in the same area, your network is not diverse at all. On the other hand, if you network with people from eight to eighty, of both sexes, with a variety of cultural backgrounds, and in different kinds of jobs in different industries, you have a very diverse network.

   0 = Looking at my network is like looking in a mirror.

   1 = My network includes mostly people like me, but it has some
       diversity.

   2 = My network has a good amount of diversity.

   3 = My network includes people from a wide variety of back-
       grounds and industries.

4 = My network includes many people from a wide variety of backgrounds, interests, and industries.

4. What's the overall quality of your network contacts? Are the people in your network experienced, with significant accomplishments? Do they have strong networks of their own? Are they well known within a professional sphere? Can they open doors for you?

0 = I like them, but they aren't movers and shakers by any means.

1 = A few people have some connections.

2 = Some people in my network really command attention.

3 = Many people in my network are at the top of their fields and very well connected.

4 = I can contact almost anyone on earth through the people in my network.

Part B: Networking Activities

5. To what extent do you actively work on building your network relationships? Do you follow up after the first meeting? Do you make sure to periodically connect with people? Do you return phone calls and answer e-mails promptly? Do you try to meet face-to-face regularly?

0 = I don't have time for all that.

1 = I try to reach out if I can find the time.

2 = I try to make time, but it's hit or miss.

3 = I consistently make time to connect with people.

4 = I make connecting with people my top priority every day.

6. How often do you actively recruit new members to your network?

0 = Never

1 = Rarely

2 = Sometimes

3 = Often

4 = All the time

7. How often do you help others in your network (both when asked for help and unsolicited)?
   0 = Never
   1 = Rarely
   2 = Sometimes
   3 = Often
   4 = All the time

8. To what extent do you leverage the Internet to build and maintain your networks?
   0 = Never
   1 = Rarely
   2 = Sometimes
   3 = Often
   4 = All the time

Add your scores together and multiply the total by 5. You'll end up with an NQ between 0 and 160. The following chart interprets your score:

0–80   **Below Average**—networking has not been on your radar screen
You need to be much more active in establishing and maintaining connections.

81–110   **Average**—nothing to brag about
You could benefit from being much more proactive.

111–140   **Above Average**—a natural networker
You are doing well, but a more systematic effort can help.

141–160   **Networking Genius!**
You know it takes ongoing effort to maintain your network.

How did you do? Are you a networking neophyte or a world-class contender? Does this self-assessment point to some areas for improvement? Remember, no matter what your score, you can always get better.

Analyzing Your NQ

Now let's dig into the details of your answers to the NQ survey. Add up your answers for part A and part B separately. Since part A assesses the strength of your current network and part B assesses the time and effort you put into networking, the scores should be similar. We should expect, after all, a direct correlation between the amount of time and effort we put into networking and the results we achieve.

If your results are out of whack (you score much higher on one part of the assessment than the other), you should take a few minutes to consider why that may be. If your score on part A indicates that you have a strong and vibrant network while your score on part B indicates that you do not put much time and effort into networking, you're in a highly unusual situation. You've gotten something for nothing. Perhaps you inherited your network, and interested family members are doing all the work to keep you included. Perhaps your spouse or a close associate is a genius networker and you are just going along for the ride. This could be a dangerous situation, and you might wake up one day and find no one bothers to return your calls any longer. Remember, it is your responsibility to build and maintain your network—no one else's.

The more likely situation, if your scores for parts A and B are significantly different, is that your part B score is higher than your part A score. In other words, your networking activities are not producing much in the way of actual results. As you read the rest of this book, you will have plenty of opportunities to consider what you might want to do differently, discarding unproductive activities for those that expert networkers have demonstrated produce results.

Also take a moment to look at your lowest scores for both parts, which can show you where you should invest the most effort. You may have a large network with strong relationships, for example, but lack diversity and quality. As you work to build your network, you can directly address those issues. Or you may discover that you rarely give back to people in your network. Over time, this can lead to people labeling you as a "user"—and cause them to distance themselves from you.

You now have a basic measure of your NQ. In the chapters that follow, you'll learn how to effectively build, nurture, and leverage your personal, professional, and virtual networks. My "Top Ten List of Successful Networking Tips" gives you a taste of what we'll cover.

In the next chapter, I'll describe my personal journey in developing my network of friends and associates. My hope is that you will not only learn from my experience but also be inspired to focus on your own experience—and the ways in which you might improve your networks.

Top Ten List of Successful Networking Tips

1. Keep networking at the top of your priority list every day.

2. Help others in your network, first and foremost.

3. Build a PBOD (Personal Board of Directors) to support your career and life.

4. Get organized—in whatever way works best for you.

5. Map your current network. It's probably better than you think.

6. Play "One Degree of Separation" to see whom you might include in your network.

7. Be interested in people and ask them a lot of questions. Networks are built through personal connections, and you never know how you might connect with someone.

8. Go for quality over quantity.

9. Diversity, diversity, diversity! The more, the better.

10. Build your personal brand.

2

Network Early, Network Often

We're all born into a network of family and friends, but sometimes we fail to see the value of these connections— or realize what they represent. We often don't realize that these natural connections with friends, family, and community can actually form the core of our networks. In the previous chapter, I asked you to estimate the size of your network universe. If you're like most people, you probably underestimated significantly, discounting people you know as "just a friend from school" or "just a cousin." My hunch is that you don't realize how connected you are. Once you're aware, you can then learn how to improve these connections and use them to your great advantage.

In this chapter, I will present my own personal networking journey as an example of how natural networking can be—and how helpful it is in life. Throughout my life, I've seen the powerful effects of a strong network. From my mother's network of friends to my father's professional networks, I've seen firsthand what a positive effect networks can have on someone's life. I've also benefited throughout my adult life from a strong network. My network has landed me jobs, opened the doors to clients, facilitated my growth and development, and enabled me to be what I am today, a successful business owner. I hope my story will provide you with a framework for analyzing and understanding your own network.

Networking Begins at Home

As is the case with most people, my network started with my family: parents, siblings, grandparents, uncles, aunts, and cousins. It then began to extend outside my family to friends of the family and my own friends. (On my dad's side, I have twenty-four first cousins, which jump-started my network in a big way.)

I think that to some degree, networking is in my blood. I learned about personal networking from my mother, JoAnn, and professional networking from my father, Ed. For decades, my mother has maintained a very large personal network of friends and family. I vividly remember her waking up early most mornings to write letters to family and friends, although I don't think she thought of it as networking. Each year, she'd send out more than one hundred Christmas cards to family members, childhood friends, friends from the neighborhoods we had lived in, work friends, and friends she met in church and at her children's schools. I was amazed at how many friends our family had and how many Christmas cards we received. She taught me that you get a lot of joy and happiness by staying in touch with people. Being a part of people's lives, even if only through annual Christmas cards, is enriching.

I also learned that connections with the people in one's network can intensify, dissipate, and then intensify again over time. My mother and father didn't see some friends for thirty years, but after they had raised their children and retired, they reconnected with many of these people. They found that not only did they still enjoy spending time with them, but the longevity of their friendships made the relationships even more special.

Life and distance can drive a wedge between even close friends, but if you can stay in touch at least once a year, you retain the potential to reestablish most relationships.

My dad taught me about professional networking. He's neither an extrovert nor a natural networker, but he's always been connected within his work communities in professional peer networks. Dad is a mechanical engineer and attended college at the General Motors Institute of Technology (GMIT). GMIT is a five-year bachelor's degree program built on an apprenticeship model. Dad always said that his experience at GMIT and the people he met during his apprentice periods were the foundations of his professional network.

He went on to work for General Foods and became a plant manager for a new dog-food plant in Topeka, Kansas. While we lived in Topeka, my dad was on the board of the local United Way and was first a member and then president of the chamber of commerce. He also joined his first professional peer network for plant/general managers. This network was run by Lyman Ketchum, my dad's boss at General Foods, who later left the company to start his own consulting firm.

This group was my first introduction to a professional peer network. I remember going to the group's meetings with my family and listening to my dad talk about the incredible value he derived from participating in this network.

Even though we moved a few times while I was growing up, I've kept in touch with many friends from grade school, junior high, and high school. So I had a pretty good-sized personal network by the time I was eighteen years old.

Beginning a Professional Network

In the introduction, I described how networking helped me get accepted to the University of Michigan. A school like the University of Michigan is what I call a "network accelerator." The

University has the largest body of alumni of any U.S. university. Just by being a University of Michigan graduate, I was automatically connected with an extensive network.

At the University of Michigan, I met a number of professors who have influenced my professional life a great deal, including business professors Robert Quinn (author of *The Master Managers*) and Dan Denison (developer of the Denison Culture Survey, a survey tool), and the highly respected management experts C. K. Prahalad and David Ulrich. Just having the university association with these prominent individuals has made establishing relationships with them easier.

Graduating from Michigan and developing relationships with these people has helped me during my entire career, as well as given me a kind of credibility by association, the "network halo effect."

Even though I had made important connections by the time I graduated from the University of Michigan in 1983, I turned

---

A **network accelerator** is a group you connect to that greatly expands your network. It can be a church, a club, a school, a professional association, or even the company where you work.

Some people dismiss the importance of such shared affiliations. The late novelist Kurt Vonnegut took note of people's natural tendency to seek and form affiliations and poked fun at this universal human trait by designating such a grouping a "granfalloon" in his 1963 novel, *Cat's Cradle*. He called a granfalloon "a proud and meaningless association of human beings." Yet it is undeniable that people place great value on their associations with others. Such associations are ubiquitous.

Consider your alma mater and the other network accelerators that may be available to you. Have you been taking full advantage of your participation in these network accelerators?

to my dad and my uncle Jack for help in finding a job. The reason for this was that these two were very well connected in their professional lives. As I described in the introduction, I was able to leverage my dad's connections into a great job at the Department of Labor.

I met a number of people at the Department of Labor who became early mentors and helped me a great deal in my career, including John Stepp and Bill Batt. I also met a lifelong friend, Ray Disch. Even though I didn't know it at the time, I was starting to create my Personal Board of Directors (PBOD). Creating a PBOD is a very important component of developing effective personal, professional, and virtual networks. We'll discuss how to create a PBOD in chapter 5.

The career guidance meetings I described in the introduction led directly to my next job. Brian Usilaner, who led the National Productivity Group at the U.S. General Accounting Office, offered me a job. I was told that I landed this job as an evaluator (a program auditor) primarily because of the writing and publishing I'd done at the Department of Labor job.

I worked at the GAO for almost four years. This job benefited my career in three major ways. First, I was exposed to a lot of great work in the areas of productivity and quality manage-

---

The **network halo effect** is the outcome associated with having well-known or respected people in your network. When you have such relationships, even if they are loose or indirect, some of these people's authority and credibility (i.e., halo) can rub off on you. It is important not to overdo it here, however. People sometimes try to take advantage of the network halo effect by name-dropping. Excessive name dropping can sometimes boomerang and diminish your own credibility.

ment. I published articles and my first book chapter on these topics (with Brian Usilaner and others) and became a budding expert on employee involvement systems and innovative performance reward systems.

Second, because all GAO work has to be sponsored by a congressperson or congressional committee, I had the opportunity to meet Senator Al Gore, who, at the time, was the head of the Senate Governmental Affairs Committee. Even more important, I became friendly with his legislative director, Thurgood (Goody) Marshall, Jr., the son of the late Supreme Court justice Thurgood Marshall.

Third, I was accepted into a graduate program at the University of Southern California (USC), which had part of its public administration school in Washington, DC. The GAO paid for part of my tuition.

> **TIP**▸ Try to get published with your mentors. It's a huge credibility builder. I've made a point of getting published with almost all the members of my PBOD over the years.

Leveraging Advisory Boards

Because the GAO formed many external advisory boards when we were working on various projects, I was able to meet a large number of experts in management fields. These experts included Dr. Ron Stupek, professor of public administration at the University of Southern California. I coauthored articles and wrote a chapter for a book edited by Dr. Stupek called *Improving Government Performance*. This was all before I was twenty-five years old.

Whether or not you had similar advantages in your early years, you can start improving your key networks right now. Wherever you find yourself in your life, learning how to use the

Connect Effect can only advance your personal life and professional career.

Exercise 2.1: Reflect on your early career.

This exercise can take the form of simply thinking for an hour or two about your early networks and the key people in those networks. You can then design a few network "trees" like the ones in this chapter (see figure 2.1).

Or, if you're so moved, you can actually write a short personal history like mine. Whatever method you choose, the important point is to achieve a sense of history and continuity—an understanding of how you got to where you are.

Whether you generally like where you are in your life or feel that you need a major overhaul, reflecting on what got you to your present situation can be an exercise of great value.

Becoming a Professional Networker

At the young age of twenty-five, I was pretty well regarded in the areas of performance-based rewards, productivity and quality management, and team-based organizations. This knowledge base was actually not very extensive; nevertheless, the knowledge base combined with the network I'd established created what I call "orbit credibility." That is, I was somewhat credible in the areas of expertise mentioned above because I'd done research in these areas and was connected to some of the thought leaders in these areas. Most importantly, I'd actually copublished with these people.

Indeed, my orbit credibility led directly to my next job, with the Conference Board. To this day, people tell me that I'm one of the only people they know who actually got a job just by answering an ad in the *New York Times*. Of course, it helped that

Orbit credibility is what you gain by being associated with a movement, project, or area of interest. You may not be the world's leading expert, but you've gained some credibility by being a part of this area and contributing to it in some manner.

the representative from the Conference Board was impressed by my résumé.

This job turned out to be an enormous boost to my career because the Conference Board is a very well-respected business advisory organization, with members that include more than two thousand of the largest U.S. companies. I became a research associate responsible for the Conference Board's Compensation Council and also helped run the organization's Quality Council.

Working with the Conference Board's clients was my first widespread exposure to the for-profit corporate world, and I met dozens of senior executives from many of the largest companies. My network grew tremendously.

TIP ▬ When looking for a job, consider not just the pay, responsibilities, and job title. Also consider whether a job offers a platform that can bring you into contact with a wide variety of respected professionals. The networking potential of a job is *often the most important benefit* you can get, especially at the start of your career.

An Entrepreneur Is Born

By the time I took the job at the Conference Board and moved to New York, however, I'd already been bitten by the entrepreneurial bug. While I was at the GAO, I had started working with a colleague on a software start-up. After eighteen months, I decided to leave the Conference Board to pursue this business venture full-time.

Our company, Insync Corporation, focused on developing a software program for designing, analyzing, and presenting data numerically and graphically from all types of surveys. Our first product, the Organization Manager, had an organization and employee survey imbedded within the software and sold for $1,495.

In the process of establishing Insync, I started to actively leverage the network I'd developed. For example, the survey we licensed for the Organization Manager came from Dutch Landen, a former General Motors executive I'd met while at the GAO. I became close friends with Dutch and his wife, Gayle, and I spent a good deal of time with them, often sleeping on their couch, while we developed the program. Dutch became a member of my PBOD and has had a profound impact on my thinking and worldview ever since.

As all entrepreneurs do, I tapped into everyone I could to help get the business off the ground. The first capital we raised came from family and friends, and our first office was a sublet from a friend who ran a public relations firm in Washington, DC. We arranged for product endorsements from the management experts I met while at the GAO. Once the program was developed and ready for market, our first customers were from the contacts I'd made at the Conference Board. We even sold a copy to the GAO.

Even though our software won awards like the HR (Human Resources) Product of the Year from *Human Resources Executive* magazine, Insync ultimately failed because my partner and I had no real business experience or education. In spite of our useful networks, we really had no clue about how to sell, market, manage cash flow, or establish strategic partnerships.

While we learned a lot very quickly, we made too many mistakes early on that we could not overcome.

It was time to look for a job. This search led me to my previous boss at the GAO, Brian Usilaner. Brian had left the government to work for a survey research consulting firm in New York City founded by David Sirota (Sirota & Alper Associates, Inc.). At age twenty-eight, I was hired as a senior consultant.

I worked at the firm for two years, but I chafed at having a boss after experiencing the freedom and excitement of running my own business. So when the opportunity arose, I jumped at the chance to try building my own business again.

Leveraging Business Partnerships

Interestingly, this opportunity came from a very large corporation: Phillips Electronics. Phillips asked me to develop a CD-I (compact disk-interactive) training program on Total Quality Management (TQM) that imbedded Insync's Assess-TQM survey within it. I took this opportunity to one of the small boutique consulting firms that was a distributor of Insync's software (which I was still selling as a side business). I asked the company's founder, Bob Shea, if he'd like to partner and develop this CD-I program. He said yes, and we reorganized Insync as a fifty-fifty partnership between the two of us.

I chose to partner with Bob because I perceived him as a "big-business man." He had worked in sales for IBM, had been senior vice president of sales for Paradigm Corporation and vice president of sales for MCI, and had been the CEO of a small technology company. Based upon my prior experience, I concluded that, while I was a pretty good product developer and had some subject-matter expertise, I still didn't know how to sell except by leveraging my limited network.

Bob and I ran our company for eight years, from 1993 to 2001. The early Internet years were a very exciting time to be in the computer software business. We leveraged the Insync survey software, adding a professional services consulting arm to our core business of selling off-the-shelf software. We also built expertise in developing computer-based training programs.

Our major business innovation (which was Bob's idea) was forming a strategic partnership between Insync and two other development firms—one focused on multimedia programming, the other on software programming. We called this alliance "Learning Technologies Group" (LTG), and we ultimately changed the name of Insync to LTG.

TIP ⊢ Business alliances and partnerships can be a very powerful way to create a larger value proposition (i.e., deliver a bigger solution) to the marketplace. They can also be a way to rapidly expand one's business network.

The LTG alliance was able to bring more than fifty employees to bear on a client project and to land projects with developmental budgets of up to $2.5 million. The LTG business partnership, at its height, had more than $6 million in annual revenues. The firm's clients included Drexel University (we created Drexel Online, one of the first university-based, Web-based course curriculums), McGraw-Hill Online Learning, Hewlett-Packard, Lucent Technologies, and Simon & Schuster (New York Institute of Finance Online).

While running LTG, I also got involved in running a peer-to-peer network for plant managers and general management called "Metamorphosis 2000." This network was founded by a former colleague of my dad's, Bill Easter. Bill was working as a management consultant and founded Metamorphosis 2000 with some of his clients and other contacts. At its height, the network had more than twenty-five members.

During these years, my personal network grew a great deal, and I met many people that are important members of my PBOD today. For example, I met Marty Maleska (then president of the International Business and Professional Group at Simon & Schuster), Bill Storts (then a managing partner at Accenture), Rich Silton (then CEO of Silton-Bookman Systems), Larry Alexander and Cedric Crocker (both then at Jossey-Bass Publishers, an imprint of John Wiley & Sons), and Brian Flynn (then a principal at the Investment Group of Santa Barbara). Marty, Bill, and Brian are on the board of my current company—Executive Networks—while Rich is the COO/CFO. Larry and Cedric have published four of my books over the last three years.

The Business Model

After the dot-com crash in 1999, it was apparent that LTG was not going to survive as a stand-alone company. My partner decided to retire, and we restructured the business with me as the sole owner. I began to tap into my network to find a buyer for LTG, which led to a contact at the Concours Group (a mid-sized management consulting firm), and within six months I had sold LTG (for stock) to Concours. I then became the head of Concours's learning services practice area.

At Concours, I studied the firm's business model, which combines consulting, research, and peer-to-peer executive networks. We formed one of the first networks for chief learning officers and conducted many groundbreaking research studies (which led to another book).

My network took another quantum leap forward at Concours, in terms of both people within the firm and contacts at client companies and academic institutions. These included

- Etienne Wenger, a leading authority on communities of practice
- Lynda Gratton, professor at the London Business School
- David Garvin, professor at the Harvard Business School
- Mark Sullivan, director of corporate learning, Honeywell
- Steve Kerr, chief learning officer, Goldman Sachs
- Ray Vigil, chief learning officer, Humana
- Frank Bordonaro, former chief learning officer, Prudential Financial

In spite of all I was learning and the great contacts I was making at Concours, my time there reinforced my earlier conclusion that I was unhappy as an employee. For whatever reason, I seemed to be a born entrepreneur.

After a year, I made the decision to leave Concours. But instead of starting a new company from scratch as I'd done twice before, I decided to buy a company that I could build. I knew from experience how incredibly difficult it is to build a business up to a critical mass starting from just a concept, especially when there is no start-up capital or large client to build with.

I developed a set of criteria for evaluating potential acquisitions, including brand, client list, intellectual property, and cash flow. After working solo and failing to secure a deal with two different companies recommended by consulting firms, I decided I needed help. I again tapped into my network and reconnected with Rich Silton, whom I had known in the early nineties. Rich had sold his company and was now helping people buy and sell small companies.

Rich helped me develop a plan of action for approaching a company and coached me expertly through the entire process. At this time I was also finishing a book project (*Corporate Learning: Proven and Practical Guidelines for Building a Sustainable Learning Strategy*) with Frank Bordonaro, who knew that I was looking for a company to buy. He suggested that I contact Jim Bolt, who ran the consulting firm Executive Development Associates, Inc. (EDA). I called Jim and introduced myself, and he invited me to visit him in Crested Butte, Colorado, for a chat.

The only reason Jim agreed to meet with me, I think, is because of my relationship with Frank, whom Jim respected, and the fact that both of us went to the University of Michigan. Once again, this reveals the importance of the Connect Effect. People are much more inclined to give you the time of day if they have some connection with you (as Jim did with me through Frank and our common status as University of Michigan alumni).

I traveled to Crested Butte and met with Jim. As it turned out, we knew many people in common because Jim worked with a lot of the people in my network (especially the University of Michigan and USC professors) as part of the custom executive-development initiatives he designed and delivered for major corporations. We also bonded because Jim ran a number of peer-to-peer executive networks, and I'd had quite a bit of experience running these networks in my career to date. Jim and I, with Rich Silton's help, negotiated my purchase of EDA, which was culminated on October 28, 2003.

EDA's Networks

As a networker, buying EDA was like finding the Holy Grail because Jim is one of the most networked people I've ever met. Jim founded EDA in 1982 and since that time has built an enormous network of contacts inside and outside of industry. EDA's client list is amazing: the firm has worked with more than fifty of the Fortune 100 companies.

In addition, at the time I bought EDA, Jim was running three peer networks with more than 80 members. To top it off, EDA has a contact database of 2,500. By buying EDA, I was able to grow my network exponentially, and with Jim's goodwill and support, I've been able to establish my own relationships with most of his network.

The final chapter in my networking journey to date is about how Jim and I have worked over the past three years to transform EDA from a consulting firm that had a few peer networks to a peer networking firm. We've grown the number of EDA networks from three to ten and currently have more than 250 members from over 200 organizations worldwide. This growth has added another layer to my network, which continues to grow every day.

Our goal is to be the world leader in executive peer networks for the human resources community, and we're well on our way to accomplishing this objective. In early 2007, we sold EDA's consulting business so we could focus 100 percent on the networking business. The firm is now called Executive Networks, Inc.

Join My Network

I even met the publishers of this book through my network. Richard Leider, a leading life coach and bestselling Berrett-Koehler author—who also happens to be a close friend of Jim Bolt's—introduced me to his Berrett-Koehler contacts.

And now, through this book, I have connected with you. Books have traditionally been tools for networking, first among learned people, then among all who could read. In the last decade, computer technology and the Internet have vastly expanded our networking capabilities. With that in mind, I invite you to meet me virtually at my Web site: http://www.the connecteffect.com.

When I reflect back on my network (see figure 2.1), I am truly astounded. I see how it started with my mother and father, then spread over the years to encompass a wide variety of people, many of whom have achieved significant accomplishments in life.

In the following chapter, I will offer some guidelines on how you can go about growing your network.

Exercise 2.2: Reflect on your career up to the present.

What got you where you are? Who helped you? Who is helping you now? Who are you helping? What are your goals? How can your personal network help you accomplish these goals?

As in exercise 2.1, you can write out your answers, make network trees, or simply reflect for a few hours. The important point is that you achieve a sense of history and continuity in your life and your networks. This will help you retain what is valuable in your personal and professional life—and change what needs changing.

In addition, understanding how you got to where you are will help to highlight what worked and what didn't work. It will also allow you to focus on who helped you, which people make up your network, and which people are key to your success. How are you employing the Connect Effect right now?

Figure 2.1 Mike's Networking History

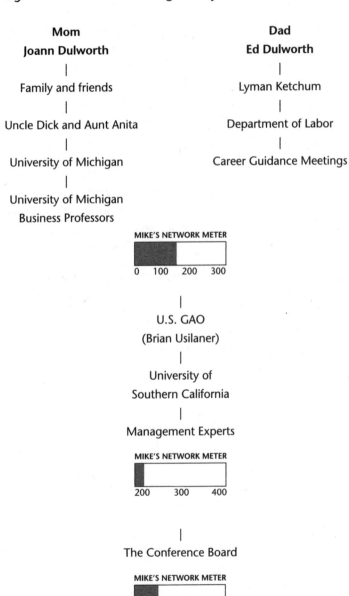

Mom	**Dad**
Joann Dulworth	Ed Dulworth
|	|
Family and friends	Lyman Ketchum
|	|
Uncle Dick and Aunt Anita	Department of Labor
|	|
University of Michigan	Career Guidance Meetings
|	
University of Michigan Business Professors	

MIKE'S NETWORK METER

0   100   200   300

|

U.S. GAO
(Brian Usilaner)

|

University of
Southern California

|

Management Experts

MIKE'S NETWORK METER

200   300   400

|

The Conference Board

MIKE'S NETWORK METER

200   300   400   500

Figure 2.1 *(continued)*

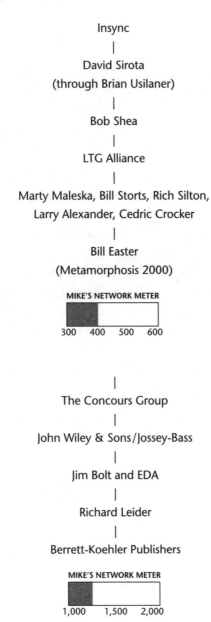

Insync
|
David Sirota
(through Brian Usilaner)
|
Bob Shea
|
LTG Alliance
|
Marty Maleska, Bill Storts, Rich Silton,
Larry Alexander, Cedric Crocker
|
Bill Easter
(Metamorphosis 2000)

MIKE'S NETWORK METER

300   400   500   600

|
The Concours Group
|
John Wiley & Sons/Jossey-Bass
|
Jim Bolt and EDA
|
Richard Leider
|
Berrett-Koehler Publishers

MIKE'S NETWORK METER

1,000   1,500   2,000

3

Building
Your Network

Most people are not very good networkers. I've come to this conclusion by talking with and watching the thousands of people I've come into contact with over the past twenty-five years. I also know that people can become better networkers by following a few simple steps. And these guidelines are not what you read about in most books on networking—for example, "the five steps to working a room" or "get out there and join a lot of groups." My advice and guidance, I hope, is much more practical and straightforward and can be weaved into a person's daily life without becoming too time-consuming. Becoming a better networker is not rocket science, but it does require some different behaviors and actions than most people exhibit or practice.

In chapter 1, I described strong, powerful networks as having four key qualities: (1) quantity, (2) relationships, (3) diversity, and (4) quality. What do you get when you have a network with all these qualities? The tagline I use for my networking business sums it up: "The right people, the right conversations, the right time."

I think this is a powerful phrase because it encapsulates so much about having an effective network and being an effective networker. Having the right people in a network should be everyone's first priority. The quality of one's network trumps the quantity every time. Does your network have high-quality individuals in it? Is it a diverse group of people in terms of age, race, nationality, gender, occupation, and so on? One of the best ways to tell if you have a high-quality network is if positive unexpected events occur because of your network.

Knowing the right people won't get you very far if you can't have the right conversations with them. You need to have enough of a relationship with people so that you can move beyond idle chatter. If you have a personal challenge, can you have a conversation with a trusted friend or mentor? If you have a business challenge, can you tap into the expertise of a knowledgeable peer? Probably the best way to get a feel for this issue is by evaluating past conversations with your network members. Were you able to have the right type of conversation with your network members, whether this conversation was via an e-mail, on the phone, or in person? If you've been frustrated by the quality of the advice and guidance you've received from your network, this may be an indication that your network is not as good as it could be.

Finally, timing is everything, so "the right time" is the last critical component of a successful network. If it takes more than twenty-four hours to hear back from someone in your network, you've not established the right type of relationship with that person in order for the right conversation to occur at the right time. The right people, the right conversations, the right time—this is the mantra of a powerful network.

The purpose of this chapter is to offer you guidelines for developing your network so that you can have the right conversations with the right people at the right time. We assessed your NQ, or networking quotient, in chapter 1. Here, I will explain in more detail how to map your current network and then offer guidelines for building it.

Understanding Your Network

Your current network, no matter how big or small, is a key tool for you to use in growing the connections you have. And to use it effectively, you must understand who is in it, who is closest to you, who is more peripheral, who needs more attention, and who is owed favors or needs your help. So the first step to take is to map your network using one of the approaches discussed in the box entitled "Mapping Your Network." Once you've mapped your network, you can start appreciating it, analyzing it, and assessing it—and then move on to building it, not as a one-time event but as a lifelong journey.

If you have taken the time to map your network, you have a pretty good idea of who's who. That's a good start, but if you want to use your network to grow your network, it helps to go a little further.

First, go through your network and identify the members as *business-card traders* (you traded cards but can hardly remember where or when), *acquaintances* (they know who you are and will probably return a call), *personal contacts* (they'll do a favor if you ask), or *close friends* (you can count on them when the chips are down).

Next, identify your top contacts, not in terms of their relationship with you, but in terms of their quality, their experience, their accomplishments, and their own networks. Who are the stars who can open lots of doors? Who has the ability to confer orbit credibility as discussed in the previous chapter?

Finally, figure out whom you want to upgrade. In other words, for those who are not yet personal friends, whom do you want to become closer to? A business-card trader may have made an impression and you neglected to follow up. Do you want to upgrade that person to an acquaintance? Do you have acquaintances who deserve to become personal contacts or friends? Make a list of all these people. If your list is long, you

Mapping Your Network

There isn't one set way to map your network. Here are a few different approaches you can take:

1. *Personal networking journey.* This approach asks you to write out your networking history from birth to the present in a chronological time line in the form of a narrative, just as I presented my network journey in the previous chapter:

   - Start with your parents (the first two nodes of your network).
   - List the members of your immediate family and your extended family.
   - Recall your family friends and the friends you've made, starting as far back as you can remember.
   - List classmates and teachers from grade school, high school, college, and graduate school.
   - Write down colleagues and bosses from the jobs you've held.
   - Describe people you've met at church, through clubs, and through any other groups you belong to.
   - List people you've met along the way, whether on an airplane, on a bus, or on the street.

   I like this particular approach to mapping your network because it puts all of your network members into a context—that is, where you met them, how important they've been to your life and career, and so on. This method also shows you how networks build over time and build organically. You'll probably also realize that your network is larger than you thought.

2. *Address book.* This approach asks you to fill out an address book (whether online or on paper) with information for all

of your network members. Most likely, you already have an address book of one type or another, but it probably does not have all of your network members listed. So start at A and go to Z, and see how many people you actually know.

3. *Tree diagram.* This approach can be used in conjunction with the personal networking journey described above. The idea is to start with the first two nodes of your network (again, your parents) and to list your network in a tree diagram. The powerful aspect of this method is that it'll show you who is connected to whom. Did you meet someone in your network through a friend, a colleague, or a casual acquaintance? Remembering these connections can be valuable when you look to tap into the power of your network because you'll understand the origins of the connections and be able to refer back to the diagram time and time again. This visual depiction of your network will also help you to quickly identify a critical person in your network, especially if you clearly label the various branches of the tree diagram. You might consider using one of the many software programs available for creating tree diagrams.

4. *Spreadsheet.* This approach allows you to create categories of information about your network members and to easily expand the information stored in these fields over time. If you put one name in each row, for example, you can have column names (or fields) for information such as network members' contact information, where and when you met them, when you've contacted them, what their areas of expertise are, and personal information on them such as birth date, children's names, and so on. The obvious limitation to this approach is that you need to constantly update the information manually, which takes a lot of discipline and time.

►

5. *Software database.* This approach is very similar to using a spreadsheet, but the organization of the information can be much more flexible, and if properly constructed, the database can be automatically updated with information from other sources. Many services exist on the Web that are essentially database tools for building and maintaining your network contacts. Some, of course, go further and link your database of contacts to other databases so that you can leverage the networks of others.

6. *Automated web tools.* A new breed of networking tools is emerging that uses software agents to gather information on people in your network via your Outlook contacts, your e-mail messages, your cell phone directory, and other sources. The tools automatically compile this information and help you organize and maintain it. Some also provide you with intelligence on your network—such as the last time you contacted a network member or the strength of your relationship with a network member—or alert you to an upcoming birthday of a network member. These tools will improve a great deal over the next few years and will help you more easily build, maintain, and leverage your networks.

may want to prioritize it and focus on the top five or so names. Later on, we'll look at ways to upgrade people, which just amounts to strengthening your relationships with them.

Network-Building Guidelines

You don't have to be an outgoing person or a social butterfly to network. In fact, social butterflies are not necessarily good networkers. (They often don't make meaningful connections and may not follow up.) As I said above, building your network is not rocket science. In fact, it is pretty simple and straightforward. To build your network, you need to plan for it and take care of it.

Plan for Networking

Networks don't happen by accident or grow spontaneously. You've got to plan for networking on a regular basis. Don't tell yourself that you are too busy. A little forethought can go a long way. Make plans to attend a meeting or conference. Make time to reach out to people. This is what Barbara Howes (who is vice president of learning and development at the Walt Disney Company and a member of Executive Networks' Chief Learning Officer Forum) told me when I asked her what the most important keys to successful networking are:

> You actually have to plan for it. You have to want to network and want to nurture that network. These are things people forget about. They might have cast a wide net of acquaintances, but they're not truly networking. One isn't leading them to another; they've just got a lot of business cards in their wallet. The key is, you have to want to network. You have to want to be in somebody else's network as well. So, be open to idea sharing or introducing folks to others they may find interesting or valuable to know. You have to make time for it. You have to actually plan this and make the effort to send a personal note or an e-mail or just to stay current on their contact information.

You must have your network in place before you really need it, Michael Drapkin emphasizes, and you need to plan to make that happen. Michael and I have kept in touch over ten years, ever since we were introduced by a mutual friend. As a classical musician and the head of his own technology firm, he networks in two different spheres. He told me, "You should always set aside a certain amount of time every week for networking because you need to have the network going before you actually need it. Your network has to be active. If you wait to activate a network after you have some specific need, it's going to be much more difficult."

Sometimes people say they just don't have the time to network—they are too busy. I think that is just an excuse when the actual problem is poor planning. Being busy is never a good reason not to network, according to Joanne Black. When I was doing the research for this book, I was told I had to meet Joanne because she is such a great networker. And she is: although she is extremely busy, she made time to talk to me. She shared a wealth of advice with me, which has helped enrich many aspects of this book. "I know everyone is super busy," she said, "but like anything else, just put it on the calendar." Joanne thought for a minute and added, "One of the things I do when I want to attend something is to pay for it because then I know I'm going to show up. If I say, 'Oh, I'll think about it and maybe do it later,' it rarely happens—because it's not on the calendar." John Zapolski thinks people can make too much out of being busy: "A lot of times we get into our routines and we get busy and we forget that there are just really small investments that need to be made to just maintain your ties."

Tammy Erickson, who was my boss when I worked at the Concours Group, offered the following advice: "One tip I would offer if it's difficult for you to network is to put yourself in a process where networking will have to occur. I think one of the great advantages, for example, for a program such as the ones that Concours runs is that it's virtually impossible not to network. You're there; the events are carefully constructed so that there are opportunities to get to know other people both on a professional and on a social level. They're relaxed so that those kinds of relationships can form. They're provocative so that new ideas can be discussed." And of course, you have to intentionally join such groups and place their meetings on your calendar.

TIP— Take a look at your calendar for the next several weeks. Do you have any events scheduled primarily for networking? Have you set aside at least a few blocks of time for the care and feeding of your existing connections through phone calls, notes, or meetings? Your calendar can be very revealing of your actual priorities as opposed to your good intentions.

Take Care of Your Network

Taking care of your network isn't complicated or difficult. It involves four key ingredients:

- ► Building relationships
- ► Giving back or giving first
- ► Recruiting new people
- ► Being sensitive

Having a strong, vibrant network is all about how you treat people. Let's look at each of these key ingredients in turn.

Building Relationships. As Joanne Black told me, there's nothing mysterious about building networks: "It's about establishing relationships and getting to know people." Jim Kouzes agreed: "It's all about relationships." And good relationships depend on trust, he added: "The underlying factor like in any relationship for me is trust. For example, take the Learning Network [Marshall Goldsmith's organized network.] People have become, over time, very self-disclosing in that group about not only professional but personal stuff that's going on in their lives, whether it's health issues or business issues." And talking to people on a deeply personal level can occur only if a bond of trust exists. Trust means being discreet: you keep confidences and don't pass on gossip. It means keeping your word. It means being responsive. It means being honorable and not taking unfair advantage of information others share with you. "Trust can't be taken for granted," Jim said. "It always has to be nurtured."

You can't build relationships with people if you never connect with them. You've got to stay in touch. I've known Jim for over fifteen years. (One of my earlier companies developed the PC software that automated *The Leadership Challenge* survey assessment based on Jim's bestselling book.) I make it a point to stay in touch with him, and we try to get together for lunch at least once a year. As Bill Morin said, "Networking is keeping your network alive and well and fresh and current. We recommend that you are always dropping little notes to people from time to time, that you are letting them know things are going well or you're available to chat with them on something, or just constantly thinking of it as your mailing list, your contact list, and you've got to work at it all the time. Every day I walk in the office and call five or six people on our contact list—just call them out of the blue. I have been doing that for years because I'm aware you can lose position and lose recognition so quickly." If you have trouble staying in touch with people, follow Joanne Black's advice and set aside time on your calendar.

This does not mean that you can build relationships by "sending two-sentence e-mails or reaching out constantly or updating your Rolodex," according to Rob Cross. "I think the problem with so many of these books [on networking] is that they're treating it as a surface-level activity. So many of them fall into this trap of creating a massive network of loose relationships as opposed to a well-invested one." Rob thinks it is etter to have a smaller network of close relationships large one of tangential connections. "What the smaller, be.. invested network is good for is that it tends to bring you opportunities and it tends to be there when things aren't going well." The message is clear: focus on building quality relationships, not quantities of relationships.

Giving Back or Giving First. As a skilled networker, you need to see that all the people in your network achieve success. As Marshall Goldmsith explained in the introduction: "To me, a key to networking is not focusing on what you can get—the key to networking is focusing on what you can give. My general philosophy is very simple. Find great people, give them things, and work on a relationship where they try to give me as much as I give them."

The idea of giving back or reciprocity came up again and again in my interviews. Here are some typical comments:

- ► "If somebody does me a favor, I want to do them a favor, and vice versa." (Jim Kouzes)

- ► "If you're going to be in a relationship, add value rather than always asking for something. A lot of networking is one-way, which is sort of the hot button for me. There needs to be reciprocity first of all." (Richard Leider)

- ► "I don't approach networking with an expectation that I'm going to get something out of this personally. It's really more of an opportunity to participate and be generous in sharing your own contacts with other people or [sharing] your own expertise. Expect to give more than you get." (John Zapolski)

- ► "You must give back to the relationship in some meaningful way and there has to be a real exchange of value for a network relationship to be worthwhile." (John Foster)

The key to reciprocity is having a level of awareness about how you behave with other people. We've all come across people who are so focused on themselves that they really can't see how others react to them—and they don't realize how self-centered they seem. If you find yourself constantly asking for favors instead of offering help, it is time to do a little soul searching. "Probably the most important thing," Barbara Howes told me, "is you have to be a good network member yourself. You have to be available for people" when *they* need help.

Part of being available to people is to let others know about your background and interests. (This involves building your personal brand, which I'll discuss in detail in the next chapter.) When people know about you, what you're good at, what connections you have, then they know how you might be able to help them. If you are always pumping others for information but not disclosing much about yourself, you aren't creating balanced relationships. Here is how IDEO's John Foster put it when we talked: "I also think it's important to have a point of view and some sense of self-awareness and aspiration so that others know how to connect to you. If people know what I'm interested in, they may have more of a desire to stay connected to me, so I become 'sticky.'"

TIP—Be open about who you are, what interests you, and what your goals are. The more people know about you, the more they are able to help.

Recruiting New People. How do you keep yourself fresh and interested (and interesting) year after year? How do you continue to grow and develop long after you've mastered the basics of your professional role? The answer is to expose yourself to new situations and new opportunities. And the best way to do that is to refresh your network with new people who bring new dimensions to your network. Rob Cross puts it this way:

> Exactly at points where leaders or others need better connectivity, new insights, innovative thinking, new opportunities, and things that keep them fresh and making good decisions, they're hearing the same voices over and over again. We know that people who fight that tendency off and continue to bridge out even when they don't see the immediate opportunity tend to do much better. Over their career, they're paid more, they're more mobile, and they advance more rapidly. My work shows they're more likely to be in the top 20 percent.

One way to meet new people is to ask people in your network to make introductions for you. Introductions are the most natural way to meet. Michael Drapkin reminded me of how we met: "You and I met because I used to work at Lehman Brothers. We had a common friend in Andy Bergen, and Andy thought, 'Gee, you two guys should meet.' He made an introduction, you and I met at some bar in Manhattan, and we established a relationship. And we stayed in touch, so there's that personal-introduction acquisition mode."

Joanne Black said that to meet new people, you should "take a look at people you already know and know well. There are hundreds of different categories of people who could be sources of referrals." People you have done business with, for example, are great resources for new business opportunities. "The most underleveraged, overlooked source of referrals are current clients. You know, the current clients are thrilled to be referrals for us, but we're just not asking. We just assume we've done great work, so of course they'll refer us. Well, yeah, sometimes they do. But I only count on what I bring about. I don't wait for the phone to ring."

But clients aren't the only ones who can refer us to new people, Joanne said: "Let's not forget all the other categories of people who could be referrals: our peers, our colleagues, our vendors, the associations we belong to, our neighbors, people we meet on airplanes. It is not just about who these people are—it's about who they know."

Joanne said that meetings, associations, and other network accelerators are also effective avenues for meeting new people. Unfortunately, people often do not use these accelerators very effectively, and they are often too impatient:

> I think there's been a lot of misuse of that word, what people typically call "networking," meeting people at different events. If someone belongs to a variety of professional associations or goes to hear a speaker . . . or goes to monthly meetings, which is pretty typical, what they need to do is find a group or two that they really like and connect with and show up regularly and volunteer so people get to know you in a different capacity. Attending events once in a while and saying "Oh, that group didn't do anything for me" is not going to work. A lot of people go into these gatherings thinking they need to do business rather than looking at how they can get to know people and help others. The goal should be to learn something and to connect with other people. And then, if you've connected with people in a way that you think you might have some information to share or you think they're interesting or for some reason there's a spark and you like them, then you set up a time to meet afterwards. But it doesn't happen overnight, especially when you're new in a group.

If you have identified someone you want to meet, you can sometimes bypass introductions and meetings and go for the direct approach. Often, just picking up the phone works. Jeff Rosenthal (a search consultant with Russell Reynolds) and I meet every six months or so to trade possible contacts. He told me, "Sometimes I've called people just to say 'I respect what you do.' I clearly say up front, 'Here's why I'd like to meet with you.'" The point is to be clear about why you want to meet. Bill Morin told me that meeting new people is not about chatting. It's all about "being specific. Being open, straightforward, when requesting information or ideas. Realizing it's not a cathartic experience when you meet with someone or chat with them on the phone; it's specific. Ask, 'Who do you know at Acme?' 'Who do you know at XX business?' Don't say, 'Gee, can you help me?' That's too general, too wide open. Most of us just don't have the time to think for the other person."

People really appreciate the direct approach. They're often willing to help, if they know what it's about. If you want to meet someone, you need to have a well-defined reason. Nothing turns busy people off more than pointless networking. "I can't tell you how often people come up and give me their card as if I should want it," Richard Leider told me with considerable heat. "And it's not that they're not nice people. What am I supposed to do with it? What exactly are you asking for? What is your request or what is your offer when you're networking? More than half the time I don't know what they're asking of me. I know they want me to either send them business or endorse their work or do something. But they don't say. And so I think it's more honest and it works more effectively if one is transparent. . . . What is it you want, or what is it you're offering?"

Of course, meeting new people is only the starting point. If you really want to build a relationship with someone so that he or she is at least an acquaintance or personal contact and not just a business-card trader, you have to follow up. As I said before, quality trumps quantity every time. When you meet a new person, "the initial handshake is the beginning of what could be a very durable long-term relationship," Patricia Franklin told me, "but it relies on excellent follow-up." Patricia is the chief learning officer for Vistage International, which is a professional networking company that has 13,500 members in fifteen countries and is the world's largest CEO membership organization based on revenue. So she knows whereof she speaks: "Let's say you go to a fantastic networking function and you walk away with a fistful of business cards, but you don't do anything with them. And weeks go by, and suddenly you really feel like you might need to follow up, but you can't because you have lost the context. You can't remember what you spoke to somebody about. So methodical, logical follow-up is key." When people give you their cards, she said, "write down on the back of the card what it is that you're going to be doing for them as a reason to follow up, or what they're going to be doing for you as a reason to follow-up."

TIP ─ When trading business cards with someone new, follow up promptly with what you want or what you are offering.

In addition to following up, you need to be patient. Relationships take time to develop. You are not going to go from a business-card trading relationship to a personal friendship overnight.

Being Sensitive. Finally, effective networkers are sensitive of others' busy schedules. "Be very, very sensitive to another person's time," Bill Morin advises. "Get to the point." Don't think you should take up time chatting about families with people unless they're personal friends. "I would recommend someone not having a networking interview or chat of more than five to ten minutes. I'm talking about a telephone contact. Now, if the person says, 'Come on in,' I would still plan that for twenty minutes, half hour max. You can always stay longer, but from an expectation point of view, I'd actually say to the person going for the interview, the networking interview chat, 'I'm only going to need twenty minutes, maybe a half hour of your time.' Allay any fear that you're going to come in and chat for two hours."

Conclusion

Building your network doesn't have to be hard work, but as we have seen, it does take planning, attention to detail, and sensitivity to others' needs. The most effective tool you have at your disposal for building your network is the network you already have. If you pay attention to the care and feeding of your existing network, use it to help you meet new people and build reciprocal relationships with them, and maintain a businesslike approach that is sensitive to others' time constraints, your network will blossom over time.

4

What's Your Personal Brand?

NODES

Do you know what your personal brand is? Did you even realize that you have a personal brand? Of course, you know companies have brands: Tiffany's is upscale, with the accent on luxury. Wal-Mart's is down-to-earth, focused on low prices. Even cities have brands: New York is the Big Apple, while Los Angeles is the entertainment capital of the world. And people have brands too—think Trump, Oprah, and Tiger Woods.

But you don't have to be a television star to have a brand. You are famous within your own network. People within your network recognize you instantly. And within your network, you have a personal brand. Your brand is, to use an older word, your reputation. It's how people know you, what they have heard about you, what they think about you.

Your personal brand isn't how you see yourself; it is how others see you. We can see this most clearly in public figures such as politicians. They work very hard to define themselves, to control the message, their personal brand—but public perceptions win out in the end. The fact is that our brands—our reputations—are rarely the result of the image we try to project but of our actual behavior (which is why people in the public

> Your **personal brand** is the sum total of the qualities people associate with you, good and bad. Your brand is primarily determined by how others see you and only partly determined by how you see yourself.

eye often get in so much trouble). Your personal brand isn't a fake persona or mask you use when you network. It is the real you as others see the real you.

To build a strong brand, you have to put yourself out there, letting people know who you are—the real you. Yes, it takes some effort, and if you're not naturally social, it can be a little risky. But people who network just to network without thinking about their personal brand, how they want to be perceived, accomplish very little. Remember how exasperated life coach Richard Leider gets with shallow networking, as I recounted in chapter 3, people just handing out business cards without really establishing any relationship. He says, "I think it's more honest and it works more effectively if one is transparent. Set clear conditions of satisfaction. What is it you want, or what is it you're offering?" Another way to put this is, what is your personal brand?

The whole point of networking, after all, is to build relationships with people who know who you are, what you're interested in, and what you can do. If you are just a networking butterfly, the most people will remember about you is a generic "nicely dressed person"—and that's only if you make it a habit to dress nicely.

TIP ⊷ To build relationships with people, let them know who you are, what you're interested in, and what you can do.

Dimensions of Your Brand

Your personal brand can be measured along two dimensions. It can vary from strong to weak, and from positive to negative:

- *Brand strength.* When people think of you, what comes to mind? If they associate a wide variety of qualities with you and have a vivid perception of who you are and your areas of interests and your strengths, then you have a relatively strong personal brand. On the other hand, if they don't have a vivid perception of you and don't have a clear idea of what your interests and strengths are, then your personal brand is weak (at least among that group of people).

- *Brand quality.* You may have a strong brand, but that doesn't mean it is positive. (Al Capone had a strong brand identity, but it wasn't good.) Your brand quality is determined by the kind of qualities people associate with you. Positive qualities such as honesty, intelligence, generosity, and reliability will contribute to a high brand quality. Negative qualities such as dishonesty, laziness, selfishness, and the like will earn you a bad reputation and a low brand quality.

If you want to enjoy a large and influential network, you need a personal brand that is both strong and positive to be the sort of person that high-quality people want to associate with. Consider the kind of referral you want people in your network to give you when they're responding to someone who asks about you or talking to someone you've wanted to meet. Do you want them to say something like this?

He (or she) is generally friendly, but I'm not sure what really interests him. Sometimes I feel he tries to take advantage of our friendship, requesting favors all the time but never offering anything in return. I once told a friend to call him for help on a topic he said he knew something about, but he wasn't much help at all. He's friendly enough—just don't count on him for anything important.

Of course you don't want people passing around that assessment of you. You would much rather hear them say something like this:

> She (or he) is a real professional interested in X, Y, and Z—a real expert on those topics. She's always happy to do a favor and really enjoys talking about the topics she is interested in. She's polite, responsible, and a real pro. She always knows what she's talking about and doesn't waste my time.

Assess Your Brand

Consider how sharp and vivid your personal brand is on the horizontal dimension below and how positive or negative it is on the vertical dimension; then place an X in the appropriate box.

Ideally, you should find yourself in the upper right-hand quadrant. If not, read on for some guidelines on how to get there.

Polishing Your Brand

You can't create your brand out of whole cloth—your brand isn't a mask you put on and take off—but you can become more aware of how you come across to others, and you can sharpen your brand by becoming clearer in your own mind about what you are interested in and what you want out of life. When we leave college, most of us aren't all that clear about our own interests, our strengths, and what we want out of life. So, naturally, our brands are more nebulous, marked primarily by our youth and (hopefully) our openness to new experiences and our quest for meaning. But as we mature, our brands should become less of a blank canvas and assume a definite shape and color. And as we advance in our career, we should establish professional expertise and credibility in some area and become known among our circle. As you build your network, you must always keep your personal brand in focus by asking yourself some critical questions:

- What is my identity? (What is my mission?)
- Am I credible?
- What is my story?
- Do I reciprocate?

Let's look at why each of these questions is so important.

What Is Your Identity?

You can polish your personal brand by being careful in how you present yourself and explicit in explaining your identity. Marshall Goldsmith works consciously to maintain his personal brand and as a result has been profiled in the *New Yorker*, the *Wall Street Journal*, and elsewhere. "In terms of a personal brand," Marshall told me, "the first thing is to have a clear mission and identity. My mission is to help successful leaders achieve a positive long-term change in behavior for themselves or people on their teams. I know what it is. If somebody asks, 'What do you do?' Well, that's what I do. Peter Drucker said, 'Your mission should be something you can put on a T-shirt.' A clear, simple, focused mission and a clear identity. Don't try to be everything to everybody."

TIP—Define your mission in a short, clear sentence that will fit on a T-shirt.

Are You Credible?

Your personal brand must begin with who you are and what you do. And it should be based on real substance, not hype. According to Marshall,

> The hardest part is building credibility. The way you build credibility is you speak, you write, and you make long-term investments in the brand. Most people do not make long-term investments in their personal brand because these investments don't quickly pay back any financial return.
>
> In establishing my brand, I set out to be a leading expert in the world. Being a world's expert at something is not as hard as it sounds—if you have a narrow focus. My goal was to be the world's most respected teacher at helping leaders achieve positive long-term change in behavior. So that's basically what I focused on doing: being a world's expert at what I do.

While Marshall was (and is) certainly not shy about publicizing himself, he realized the basics mattered more: whether there is substance behind the hype. He put in the time and effort to back up his claim. He has, he told me, paid his dues.

Vince Perro thinks substance matters more than marketing skills when it comes to polishing your brand. I met Vince through one of my executive directors who used to work for Vince when he led Sibson Consulting. He told me,

> I think that you can brand yourself ultimately in two ways: one is through a substantive path, and a good example is Ram Charan [the author of several bestselling management books, such as *Execution*], who writes frequently and thoughtfully and very expansively on issues of the modern corporation and business conditions; I think that's why he's got a great personal brand. And the other way is through a lot of personal marketing and self-promotion. I'm not convinced that the latter is a sustainable way to build a personal brand. I think for the typical person, your personal brand is a function of your reputation with the individuals and institutions with which you come into contact.

And this isn't based on marketing hype but your actual performance in dealing with others. Have you done the work and paid your dues? Do you keep your promises? Do you live up to expectations?

Another aspect of credibility involves being yourself, being genuine. You cannot develop a strong personal brand if it isn't about the real you. When I asked Genentech's Nisha Advani what the top keys to successful networking are, she said, "The first, to me, is just being genuine. I really try to be who I am so that will come through. I trust that when I show up as myself, and have a genuine interest in the other person, real connections will be made." Networking is first and foremost about making real connections, which means that your personal brand must be genuine and credible.

Your credibility is your most important asset in strengthening your brand—be careful never to undermine it. As Jim

Kouzes told me, "You must—if you really want to develop a network that lasts and have it facilitate the development of long-term relationships and build your credibility—present yourself in a way that you (and your mother!) would like to see reflected back five to ten to twenty years from now." Remember, you are always onstage. Careless behavior can come back to bite you very easily, especially in today's world of the Internet. (I will talk more about online behavior in chapter 9.)

Your personal credibility has to be enhanced by two other mechanisms I discussed in chapter 2, orbit credibility and the halo effect, both of which enhance your credibility through association with projects and people who are credible themselves. Marshall Goldsmith was very candid about this aspect of brand building:

> The second thing in terms of building a personal brand is to work with people who are at the top of the world. I've had the privilege of working with Richard Beckhard, Paul Hersey, with people like that. They helped me. Your chairman, Jim Bolt, is one of the reasons I am where I am in life. I have no problems with giving him due credit. Jim Bolt helped me long before I was rich and famous. So Jim Bolt helped me, Peter Drucker helped me, Paul Hersey helped me, Frances Hesselbein helped me—these are all people who helped me.

Remember Michael Drapkin, who networks in both high-tech business and classical music circles? He used the network halo effect to gain credibility in a world where he had little experience—higher education:

> When I was first getting into all of my analysis and research on entrepreneurship in music, I had no real credibility in the music higher-education community. Even though I had

chaired a program at Columbia University, it was in e-commerce and it was not in music. And at the urging of some sponsors that I had, I created a not-for-profit foundation called the Foundation for Entrepreneurship in the Arts. And I created an advisory board of various people who could give me advice and give me credibility, and I lured them onto that board by saying that they had no fiduciary responsibility and there would be no meetings. So if you go and look at the advisory board, it's a stellar group of luminaries that gave me a great deal of credibility and helped me to move my aims forward.

What Is Your Story?

We connect with others by the stories we tell. When you meet new people, they want to know who you are and why you are here. The best way to show them is not to pull out a résumé or cite a list of facts but to tell them a story that reveals who you are on a personal level. "The power of networking is in storytelling one way or another," Richard Leider told me. "People are so hungry, they're almost desperate to tell their stories, to be heard. You go into any coffee shop today and listen to the conversations on either side of you, and it's people pouring their stories out." Storytelling should focus on you, not other people—which would be essentially gossip. Marshall Goldsmith told me, "Rather than talking about other people, wouldn't it be nice if [we would] stick with our own stories. I had to have a message to deliver. I'm always working on that and trying to make it better and better, but early on, I didn't have a very good message."

Stories allow you to relate to people on a deeper level. When you have a meeting, Richard told me, "Whoever's convening it needs to start with their story, and the transparency or the honesty of that really invites the stories of others, at the end of which people say, 'This felt so good.'"

Whether you think you are a good storyteller or not, the only way to get better is to practice. There is no single way to tell a story. Tell your story in a way that works for you, and keep refining it and practicing it. Over time, you will get better and better at telling your story. Just make sure it is genuine.

Do You Reciprocate?

There's that word "reciprocate" again. In the world of networking, it just won't go away. The fact is, failing to reciprocate, to give back, can be very damaging to your personal brand. You can end up with an image that is very vivid but very negative. On the other hand, giving first can provide a tremendous boost to your personal brand. Volunteer to help without being asked. It works wonders. I've talked a lot about the importance of reciprocity already, so I don't need to go into detail here. Just remember that it can have a powerful influence on your personal brand.

Conclusion

Your personal brand is one of the most valuable assets you possess. Cultivate it, grow it, and protect it. Your personal brand is your good name, and as Shakespeare wrote,

> But he that filches from me my good name
> Robs me of that which not enriches him
> And makes me poor indeed.
> (*Othello*, act III, scene 3)

As we have seen, building your brand involves clarifying your identity and mission, establishing your credibility, learning to tell your story, and making sure you give at least as much as you receive. In the next chapter, we will look at creating another valuable asset, your personal board of directors.

Protecting Your Brand: Networking Dos and Don'ts

Networking etiquette can make or break your personal brand. You can build expertise in your field, develop a strong identity and mission, and tell a perfect story that reveals who you are, why you are here, and where you are going—but all that won't get you very far if your networking manners are lacking. Follow these dos and don'ts:

Networking Dos

1. *Do connect with all of your network members at least once a year—or even better, every six months.* (Birthday and holiday wishes are an excellent way to connect.) Absence may make the heart grow fonder, but in networking, it makes the brand grow fainter. And if you connect with people only when you need something, you'll violate the next rule.

2. *Do be reciprocal with your network members; give first and often.* No need to expand on this.

3. *Do be clear and concise in what you're asking from a network member or your network.* According to Barbara Howes, "You need to say, 'How can I be of service to you? How can you be of service to me? What do we have in common?'" People won't take you seriously if you're networking without purpose, what Barbara calls "cocktail party networking."

4. *Do ask your existing network members for referrals to people you want to meet.* This is one of the best ways to expand the quality and quantity of your network and to take advantage of the network halo effect, which can really boost your personal brand.

5. *Do behave well—be extremely polite and thankful with your network members.* If you want people to recommend and refer you, you have to earn their trust.

▶

6. *Do be sensitive about time.* As Bill Morin told us in chapter 3, effective networkers are considerate of others' busy schedules. It's a matter of being professional.

7. *Do limit your drinking.* At a networking event, pay very close attention to the amount of alcohol you're consuming.

Networking Don'ts

1. *Don't send out blast e-mails (one e-mail with everyone's name on the cc list) to your network; send individual e-mails, even if they all have the same message.* No one is flattered to be included on a list of dozens of names. And never send members of your network jokes or political cartoons unless you really know them well, including their views and beliefs.

2. *Don't turn a networking event into a sales call.* If you are constantly selling something, that activity will become part of your brand and turn people off. Nisha Advani, like many people, really tries to avoid "that bombardment of people trying to sell something."

3. *Don't use slang or swear words in a communication to your network members—or be sloppy with grammar or punctuation.* It's a matter of being professional and on your best behavior at all times.

4. *Don't burn bridges.* Jack Rosenthal told me, "No matter what occupation you're in, the world is very small. I've seen people who burn bridges have it come back to bite them."

5. *Don't gossip.* If people hear you gossiping about others, they'll assume you will gossip about them and keep their guard up when you are around. It's fine to talk about other people but only in a positive way.

6. *Don't hog the spotlight.* While it's important to tell your story, you also need to let others tell their stories. You need to show a real interest in others to build relationships.

5

Entering the Network Zone

At this point in my life, I've entered the rarefied world of the "Network Zone." There is almost nothing that I can't do or accomplish—or do better, more efficiently, and more effectively—through my network. This network has grown so extensive and deep that I can tap into it to support me personally and professionally and even leverage it to make a positive impact on society.

What can you accomplish when you're in the Network Zone? The answer is, just about anything! This book is one result of being in the Network Zone. But the Network Zone can go far, far beyond getting books written and published. When I interviewed leadership expert and bestselling author Jim Kouzes, he told me the following story:

> I remember when we interviewed Don Bennett, who was the first amputee to climb Mount Rainier. Don responded to one of our questions in a very memorable fashion. When I asked him what was the most important lesson he learned in climbing this mountain (14,470 feet, or something like that) on one leg and two crutches, he said, "You can't do it alone." He said, "I wouldn't have made it to the top of this mountain

if it weren't for my climbing team, and I wouldn't be alive today if it weren't for my family." And I think we should all remember that every day—that you can't do it alone.

When you have a team backing you, you can do just about anything—even climbing Mount Rainier on one leg and two crutches. Of course, teamwork has always been important, but it is different today. Many of the people I talked to for this book remarked on how different the experiences have been for the boomer generation as opposed to Gen X and Y. The boomers and the generation preceding them went to work for organizations and expected to stay there until retirement. To a large extent, the organizations provided ready-made networks for them. "And as a result, they tended to form very close relationships with institutions," Tammy Erickson told me. She leads the Concours Institute, a research group focusing on the changing workforce and innovative ways to shift the relationship between employees and corporations. "They're comfortable with government, very pro corporate institutions, and had the expectation that they were going to stay part of those institutions for their entire career. So networking in those cases had more to do with success within an institution as one began to move up the corporate ladder and advance in a career."

Now no one expects—or wants—lifetime employment. Today's midcareer professionals, the so-called Generation X, really don't see their careers as ones in which they patiently work their way up the corporate ladder. Moreover, growing up, they had radically different experiences from their predecessors, Tammy told me. "They grew up in a time when we were seeing divorce rates skyrocket, unemployment was skyrocketing, layoffs, reengineering, lots of change in the social fabric. They were home alone in the afternoons and, in many cases, spending the afternoon with their friends. That situation, therefore, developed a generation of people who tend to maintain and value very strong relationships with friends—in many cases, more so than even with family members and, in almost every case, more so than with corporations or institutions."

Today, we are less tethered to organizations and the built-in networks they provide. We must build our own—creating our own teams—and move into the Network Zone.

To get a feel for what being in the Network Zone is like, let's play a game called "One Degree of Separation." You've undoubtedly heard the term "six degrees of separation" to describe a scenario in which every one of us is just six people away from everyone else in the world. While this is an interesting idea, I don't find it that useful when thinking about effective networking. Connecting with six different people to get to someone you want to meet is just too time-consuming and impractical. On the other hand, thinking about whom you might get to know based on whom the people in your network are connected with is pretty straightforward. Ask your contacts whom they know and what connections they might be willing to make for you. You could radically improve the quality and quantity of your network with a few easy steps. It's also fun to see if you are one step away from any famous people. For example, my brother-in-law works for President Bill Clinton, so I'm one step away from him, Senator Hillary Rodham Clinton, and a whole host of interesting people my brother-in-law meets in his job.

You're in the **Network Zone** when you have developed deep connections with a high-quality network so extensive that you can tap into it to accomplish almost anything.

Taking Your Network to the Next Level

Do you want to enter the Network Zone? If so, I suggest that you need to develop deeper relationships; connect with an extensive, diverse array of people; and develop your own personal board of directors.

Developing Richer Relationships

We've touched on the importance of building real relationships with people, emphasizing that the quality of your relationships means more than the quantity and explaining the importance of upgrading relationships from acquaintances to friends. I'm returning to the topic here because, frankly, I think this is where most people fall short. They don't follow up enough, they don't open up enough, and they don't make a deep human connection in their networking. Rick Smith is the founder of the networking firm W50 and coauthor of *The Five Patterns of Extraordinary Careers*. He told me that most people go about networking in the wrong way. As Rick advised me, "Very few people do it well. People tend to network, or reach and nurture their network, when they need something, and that is the opposite way to be successful in building relationships."

Joanne Black also remarked on many people's poor relationship skills:

> People don't know how to interact when they go to an event. Either they'll stand on the edges of the room, like when we were in middle school and everybody was shy, or they'll hang out with the people they came with because that feels comfortable. Or they decide to blast through the room and meet as many people as possible and give you their card and get your card. That's not genuine, and any of us can recognize

that a mile away. I can spot those people at every event, and I'll run the other way because they'll ask me for my card. I won't give it to them because what will happen is you'll get an e-mail the next day, it'll be way too long, and it will say, "Great meeting you at such and such an event and here's what I do. If you know anybody who could benefit from my services, please forward this e-mail." Well, why would I?

The problem is that many people treat networking like a game, when in fact it is the exact opposite. "A lot of people," Joanne went on, "think they're having a contest about how many business cards they can collect. It's not about that at all. What it is about is meeting people and making connections."

Relationships are so important because they are the basic reason people provide help to others. Jim Kouzes, for example, told me, "I get a lot of people who'll send me an e-mail and want something from me. If I have no relationship with them, no reason to trust that person, I'm not going to be, at least initially, offering them much. I may acknowledge it and be gracious, but I'm not going to disclose myself or engage immediately with some kind of business proposition with them." Joanne Black agreed: "Referrals are based on relationships. You're not going to refer someone unless you know, like, and trust them because it's a reflection on you when you refer someone. I'm not going to refer you unless I know you personally, I know your values, I know that you do good work."

How do you move beyond trading business cards and having one-time transactions to develop real relationships with people? Here is some advice from expert networkers:

First, find common interests. As IDEO's John Foster told me. "If I meet somebody, I'm very interested in making a personal, authentic, real connection about something that we're both interested in. So I usually ask questions like, What do you do? How long have you been doing that? What are you interested in? What are you hoping to do?"

- *Have real conversations with people.* You need to get beyond saying, "Here's my card." As Joanne Black told me, "My goal when I go to a networking event is to have probably three to four substantive conversations, period. If I do that and I come away with a couple of people I want to follow up with after it, that's been a great evening." And Jim Kouzes advises, "Our initial conversations with people tend to be pretty shallow. It's only after you get through the BS that you get to the real stuff. You've got to be willing to be pretty self-disclosing."

- *Stay in touch with people, face-to-face.* Don't think an annual e-mail is going to build a real relationship. "I think it's important to spend time having lunch every now and then to connect face-to-face," John Foster told me. "There are certain people that I've worked with over the years that continue to help me create opportunities, so I stay connected with them through e-mail, and every now and then we meet for lunch or coffee or something."

- *Stay focused.* "I'm so swamped that I really don't want any more information," Rick Smith said. "I want less information, but the *right* information. And I really don't necessarily want to meet more people. I just want to focus my time on meeting the right people and having much richer relationships with those individuals. I'm much more interested in connecting with people, regardless of whether they're influential or not. And if there's a real, authentic connection, then I try to steer those relationships and those friendships, trying to figure out how can I be helpful to them." And that brings us back to our old friend, reciprocity—giving back or giving first.

► *Give back or give first.* Let's hear from Rick again: "The successful people that I've seen are always focused on 'What is it that I can do to help somebody without any expectation of return benefit?' We wrote about this in our book *The Five Patterns of Extraordinary Careers* in an area called 'benevolent leadership,' where people in the leadership are focused on the success of their peers and subordinates as much or more than they're focused on their own success. And just like the networker that's constantly going around trying to figure out how they can be helpful to other people, you basically build up this army of influential people that are indebted to you in one way or another, and sooner or later, if you really do need to cash in that chip and there's something urgent, they're more willing to help you out. But even more powerful than that, it's the times when you have no idea that they're even in a position of influence, where they go out of their way to help you in an area that you hadn't even expected."

Being in the Network Zone depends on having real relationships with people, not just hundreds of names in your BlackBerry. Ask yourself, When I reach out to people in my network, how responsive are they? If people aren't glad to hear from you when you contact them, you've got to put more thought and energy into your relationships with them.

TIP ► Don't fall into the e-mail trap. Try to connect with people in your network face-to-face at least once or twice a year.

Broadening Your Diversity

If you're in your early twenties—part of the so-called millennial generation—you probably know all about diversity. According to Tony DiRomualdo, who founded Next Generation Workplace, which focuses on understanding the practices of people-centered, high-performance organizations, millennials are "the first generation where diversity isn't a concept; it's what they live with and consider normal." If you are a member of this generation, congratulations. For the rest of us, diversity may be something we have to work at. I've talked about diversity before, but since it isn't something many people in older generations grew up with, it is probably worth spending a little more time on it here.

Diversity is important for a simple reason. People with diverse networks are more successful than those without. Jim Kouzes told me, "The first principle I tell people, and it's based on our research, is that people who have diverse, extensive, and deep networks are more likely to be successful than those people who have very narrow and shallow networks."

TIP — People with diverse networks are more successful than those without. Connect with a wide range of people.

In fact, even if you are successful, networking with diverse people can be even more important as your career progresses. Success can bring its own problems, search consultant Jeff Rosenthal told me. People become so busy, they lose touch with friends: "As people move up in an organization, they tend to pay less attention to networking and they get more isolated. I don't necessarily mean just isolated in their company; I also mean isolated in their community." Rob Cross, the researcher at the University of Virginia, said fighting isolation is important: "We've focused our research on high performers (the top 20 percent) at over fifty organizations. What the high performers seem to do is that they manage to fight off insularity. They don't allow groups to close around them so that they're trafficking the same information all the time. There's a certain category of person that continues to reach out in the belief that these opportunities will emerge, and then there's an awful lot that don't. They just kind of focus more narrowly." Richard Leider added, "Isolation is fatal in the long run."

The benefits of a diverse network are clear to those who are fortunate enough to possess them. John Zapolski of the Management Innovation Group explains how networking with a diverse group can lead to unexpected results—you can find valuable things you weren't even looking for: "Networking pulls me in all kinds of unintended directions, often leading to being in the right place at the right time with the right people."

Michael Drapkin gives a good example of the serendipitous opportunities that can come from diverse networking: "For example, in conjunction with my musical entrepreneurship activities, I joined the College Music Society, and I blindly put in a proposal for presenting a paper on an entrepreneurship curriculum that I had put together for music schools. Well, it got accepted, but when it got accepted, I was contacted by a woman by the name of Judith Coe who was on one of their committees and who was very interested in the stuff I was doing. We hit it off, and through my contacts with her, I ended up meeting a whole bunch of other people, many of which became speakers at the conference that I put on last summer in North Carolina." He suggests that you can add diversity to your network by "joining either user groups or professional associations, where you can make an enormous number of contacts."

John Foster said, "Networking is becoming more and more important as a way to navigate an increasingly complex world." And diversity is the key. As the world grows ever more complicated, you can be blindsided by events or miss opportunities if you don't have access to people who know what you don't, see the world differently, and pay attention to different things. A narrow focus can be dangerous.

Do you want the benefits of a diverse network? Don't always stay in your comfort zone. Consider opportunities to meet people in different settings, even those you are less familiar with. Meet with people who are in a completely different industry than you are in. Don't limit your networking to people in your professional life. Not only will adding diversity to your network help you better solve problems and enhance your career aspirations, it will probably make you a better, more well-rounded person.

Creating Your Personal Board of Directors

The next step in entering the Network Zone is to create your own personal board of directors. Remember how my first company, Insync, failed because my partner and I had no real business experience or education? I firmly believe that Insync would have succeeded if we had created a board of directors for the company composed of experienced businesspeople. I have learned from this experience: at Executive Networks, I have taken great care to gather the best of the best for my board of directors.

Now, if a business gets great benefits from the guidance of a group of wise, experienced people, why shouldn't this work for an individual? Well, it does! Most of the expert networkers I interviewed for this book had something like a personal board of directors, although most didn't call it by that name. Vince Perro told me, "Everybody needs sounding boards. Certainly we all have people . . . who we get to know over the years—various mentors and business colleagues from whom we seek advice—and certainly I've done that as well. I have always been fortunate enough to have . . . a variety of people who have been able to offer me personal advice about . . . career and other business-related decisions, and that's been something I've been very grateful for."

Jeff Rosenthal said, "I do have seven or eight people who have been my personal board. It changes over time a little bit, but I tend to stay in touch with people for a long, long time. I feel a lot of loyalty to the people that for whatever reason have been helpful to me and where I've built a personal relationship. So the idea that you have people who know, who trust you, who you trust, that understand you, that you can really use as that personal board of directors is a really helpful thing."

When I asked Jim Kouzes if he had a personal board of directors, he answered right away: "I do and they're not always the same individuals. One of my closest partnerships has been with my coauthor, Barry Posner. Barry is always someone that I feel comfortable talking through various dilemmas, personal issues, personal career changes, etc. He is always somebody that's been a good counselor and advisor. When I, these days, think about any kind of a personal or professional change, it's always my wife whom I turn to. I also use a group like the Learning Network and some of its particular members, like my good friend Bill Bridges, to share future aspirations and talk about the past year and, in that context, get advice."

If you stop to consider, you will probably realize that you already have an informal PBOD—a few people whose opinions you value and whose advice you seek from time to time. The purpose of a PBOD is to expand this network and work with it

---

A **Personal Board of Directors**, or a **PBOD**, is similar to a corporate board of directors. It's a diverse group of people who care about you and can provide advice and guidance throughout your life. The members of your PBOD may change over time, but some people (like your mother or a sibling) will probably remain on your PBOD for a lifetime.

in a more focused manner. Wise counsel, given at the right time, can be an invaluable asset to your personal and professional life.

Unlike a corporate board, your personal board will not get together for formal meetings. Instead, you will contact each individual for advice and discussion on a particular issue or concern when the need arises. You may contact several members or just one—whoever you feel is an expert or will have sage advice on the topic or issue at hand. Some members may give you wise counsel on your personal life, while others may be experts in your professional field.

I suggest that you limit your PBOD to six to ten members. Just like a corporate board, too many members can be difficult to engage and manage effectively. Staying in touch every three to four months with your PBOD is very important because you want members to be up to speed on developments in your work and personal life when you seek out their advice and guidance.

Choosing Your PBOD

If you mapped your network as I suggested in chapter 1, you can use that map to help you decide whom within your network you would like to have on your PBOD. I suggest that you form your PBOD from the members of your existing network because it is important to have people whom you know very well, who care about you as a person, and whom you trust enough to be candid and honest with about your life, warts and all. The questions in the box "My Personal Board of Directors" can help you think through whom you want to be on your personal board.

Once you have your list, you can contact each person, explain the concept of a PBOD, and ask if he or she would consent to this relationship. You need to be clear on what you

My concept of a PBOD owes much to Richard Leider, one of the foremost executive coaches in the world. Richard calls this personal board "My Sounding Board" and has created a booklet with this title. Richard has been kind enough to let us reproduce part of this booklet (see resource A). You can also order copies of the booklet and learn more about Richard's superb work at his Web site: http://www.inventuregroup.com.

would like from each person and describe exactly what you expect. For example, you might need your PBOD members' counsel several times a year. They might be asked to respond by e-mail, phone, or perhaps an actual meeting.

My PBOD includes my father, my wife, a mentor from my second job out of college, a career management professional, one of the members of my business board, the COO at Executive Networks, the founder of Executive Development Associates, one of my oldest friends, my best friend, and a cousin. These ten people are a mix of family, friends, and business colleagues. All are people who care about me a great deal, know me well (the good and the bad), and will provide objective (sometimes brutally honest) advice and guidance. The constant members of my PBOD have been my family and friends, while the changing members have been people in my professional network.

The formation of a PBOD gets back to the issue of network quality versus quantity. A PBOD is clearly focused on quality and can be a wonderful tool to leverage your network for both personal and professional benefit.

Just as in any network, remember that reciprocation is the key to success. If you are asked to be a member of someone else's PBOD, you will need to give this careful consideration.

Doing It Together

Upon being congratulated on yet another winning season for his New York Yankees, manager Casey Stengel blurted out, "I couldn't have done it without the team!" While this may seem obvious, what's not always obvious is that *nobody* does it without a team. Highly successful people may be gifted in certain ways, but a close look at their careers will reveal a network of support communities that helped them get ahead.

You have the ability to create this kind of community around you when you enter the Network Zone.

My Personal Board of Directors

1. Who has been instrumental in helping me in my personal life and professional challenges?

2. Whom do I turn to when faced with a daunting challenge?

3. Who deeply cares about me?

4. Who provides me with sound, objective advice and guidance?

5. Who understands me—my background, life experiences, and personality?

6. Whom can I rely on when the chips are down?

7. Whom do I consider a mentor or coach?

8. Who can help me accomplish my life and professional goals?

9. Who, within or outside my network, has a background, ideas, or experience different from my own and can help me see issues or challenges from diverse perspectives?

10. Whom do I listen to and respect?

PART TWO

Harnessing the
Power of
Different Networks

6

Networking
Peer-to-Peer

We're going to shift gears a bit now. We've been discussing ways to develop your networking skills and build your network. In the next few chapters, we're going to focus on different types of networks. The peer-to-peer networks discussed in this particular chapter bridge organizational boundaries. Chapter 7 will focus on internal organization networks, and chapter 8 will discuss communities based on a common concern or passion: communities of practice.

While, by definition, peer-to-peer networks lack an important dimension of diversity (everyone has the same occupation), the trade-off is well worth it. As Jim Bolt, wrote in a recent article in *Fast Company*, "The central idea behind the effectiveness of peer-to-peer networks is this: We all learn better, trust more, and gravitate to the shared experiences of people at our level and in circumstances similar to ours. And, there is incredible value in being able to tap into the collective experience of a group of trusted peers."[4]

When computer techies talk about peer-to-peer networks, they are referring to computer networks with no hierarchical structure: every computer is on the same footing. It's the same when it comes to people: in your peer-to-peer network, you are with your equals. One reason that peer-to-peer networks are so effective is that they create a secure, open environment that helps accelerate learning and development. The network becomes a safe harbor for participants to freely discuss issues and challenges of individual and organizational importance with peers in organizations who have very similar positions and responsibilities.

If you belong to a professional association such as the American Marketing Association, the American Society for Training and Development, or the Public Relations Society of America, you may already be a member of a peer-to-peer network. Literally thousands and thousands of professional associations cover virtually every conceivable occupation, from mechanical engineers, schoolteachers, and cinematographers to plastic surgeons, botanists, and police officers. (There is even a very large association of the people who administer associations, the American Society of Association Executives.) While many of these associations are too large and diverse to be called peer-to-peer networks, almost all have sections or divisions centered on specific interest groups, professionals, or level of experience—and these are true peer-to-peer networks. Many are also organized regionally, allowing you to personally connect with the peers in your own community on a regular basis.

TIP— If you belong to a professional society but don't do much beyond attending the annual meeting, consider becoming more involved. Look for interest groups that match your field or look for local chapters, which often meet monthly. These ready-made networks can be very valuable. Your association probably has a Web site where all this information is at your fingertips.

A **Peer-to-Peer Network** consists of people who are alike in some way—usually based on their occupation—such as certified public accountants, human resource executives, CEOs of Fortune 500 companies, or students studying political science.

Another type of peer-to-peer network is the professionally managed network, which I became acquainted with early in my career. When I worked at the Conference Board, I ran peer-to-peer networks. While running one of my first companies, I got involved in running a peer-to-peer network for plant managers and general managers called "Metamorphosis 2000." Later on, at the Concours Group, we formed one of the first networks for chief learning officers. Then when I bought EDA, Jim Bolt was already running a number of peer-to-peer executive networks—and today, that is the entire focus of my company, which is now called Executive Networks.

Rick Smith, who founded the professional network firm W50, describes his company's approach to peer-to-peer networking:

We create groups of fifty noncompetitive executives. It's invitation only, by a sector, and each of them pays a substantial annual fee to participate, which creates the funding from which we can staff a very senior team to facilitate the discussion on a year-round basis. We get the members together formally a couple times a year, and informally, there's opportunities for collaboration on a year-round basis, with dinners, conference calls, direct connections that we make between the members, and connections we make with members and nonmembers where it makes sense. And then finally, out of all of that interaction and conversation, we developed some very cutting-edge content that can then be disseminated back to the entire membership. So, in some ways, it's almost like creating a consulting offering where it's really your other forty-nine true peers that are providing you the advice and counsel, depending on what you're dealing with.

The substantial annual fee Rick mentioned is well into five figures. Why would people pay high fees to join a network when so many other opportunities are available—many that are very low cost or even free? Tammy Erickson of the Concours Group explained one reason to me. She calls it "the sorting function":

> The reality is you can network today with anybody. You can have some kind of e-mail blast to a list and you can send out all sorts of communications to people. In some ways the more interesting question is, How do you choose where to focus your networking activities? How do you choose who will be in your network? The advantage of a company like Concours is that it not only helps you with the [networking] process, but it also helps with the selection by creating peer networks that put you in contact with people that you should want to form relationships and networks with.

Whatever form of peer-to-peer networking you engage in, you should engage. Peer-to-peer networks can profoundly impact your career and produce enormous economic benefits for your work organization, as I discuss below.

How Peer-to-Peer Networks Work

Peer-to-peer networks can take a multitude of forms. They often include components such as these:

- ► *Meetings.* Typically, several meetings are held each year. Meetings might include the following elements:
  - An in-depth profile of an individual member company

- A theme chosen by the members for discussion, including an outside speaker as a catalyst for deep dialogue

- Pure networking time when each person has the opportunity to present what he or she is working on that might be of interest to the group and to get ideas, support, and recommendations

➤ *Web site.* A private Web site may be set up for communicating and networking among members in between face-to-face meetings. .

➤ *Online peer networking.* Members can send e-mails to all network members to inquire about some issue or gather information of particular interest.

➤ *Teleconferences.* Networking is typically supported by regularly scheduled teleconferences on topics of specific interest.

➤ *Research.* This component may include in-depth and pulse research projects to benchmark and identify best practices.

I recommend that you have at least one professional network, a network of peers who have job roles and responsibilities similar to your own. In this type of low-risk forum, participants usually feel far less pressure to be the "expert." They can ask questions more openly and search for answers without the political and emotional weight often present when these issues are discussed within their own organizations.

TIP ➤ Many professionals are not part of a formal or large organization. However, with the growth of the Internet, it's easy for individual entrepreneurs to find networks of peers. Simply key in your specialty on a search engine and you will find a myriad of opportunities for networking with your peers. Alternatively, you can ask colleagues to recommend a network that they use.

The Benefits of Peer-to-Peer Networks

Participants in peer-to-peer networks commonly say that these forums provide an extremely valuable developmental experience, producing tangible benefits from a personal and career perspective, as well as significant organizational benefits. Examples of this value include

- ► Accelerating innovation
- ► Reducing risk
- ► Improving the use of resources
- ► Improving quality
- ► Improving individual effectiveness and job satisfaction
- ► Advancing the field

Let's take a deeper look at each one of these benefits.

Accelerating Innovation

The speed of global change and the increasing demands of global competition require corporations to accelerate their own pace of innovation and improvement as both a defensive and an offensive strategy in their markets. Networks provide a way to accelerate information gathering, which then creates the foundation for accelerating the innovation capability of the corporation as a whole.

Dr. Richard O'Leary, director of human resources, science and technology, at Corning Inc. commented, "One of the key impacts of my network is in accelerating the speed with which you can get things done. It has accelerated the speed of our work."[5]

In some cases, network members experience this impact on a very personal basis in terms of their ability to save precious hours or even days of their own time accessing information on best practices. Deborah Swanson, national director of talent and organizational development for Sony Electronics, provides us with a dramatic example of time saving: "I was recently requested to help find a highly credible consultant to facilitate a national sales strategy session. I was able to send a request to the network for recommendations and personal references and was able to do in a few hours what would have taken a week of my time to research."[6]

Reducing Risk

Peer network participants say that the value of their network is not only in the knowledge they gain about best practices but in the opportunity to avoid corporate "worst practices." Just as in your personal life, failures are often as instructive as successes.

The strong level of trust established between network members provides a high level of openness in their dialogue that allows members to share failures so that the entire group can learn from them and brainstorm on ways to avoid them.

Improving the Use of Resources

Efficiency has always been important, but extreme global competition makes cost control and cost reduction increasingly critical for business survival and success. Peer network members often find that networks reduce their costs and improve their use of resources in a variety of ways.

First, a good peer network decreases its members' reliance on expensive consulting resources by providing them with essentially free consulting from a network of their peers. When members do need to use consultants, they avoid costs associated with poor vendor selection by pooling their experiences with a wide range of vendors.

In addition to these savings, their companies also reap both cost and revenue improvements from the greater effectiveness

of adopted best practices. Chuck Presbury, senior director of
leadership development for the McGraw-Hill Companies, Inc.,
recounts one example of how his participation in a network enabled him to save several million dollars on one decision alone:

> At my previous firm we were in the early stages of designing
> a large-scale executive and leadership development process.
> The COO of the firm was willing to build a physical facility
> (like GE Crotonville) as a focal point for the initiative. I
> posed this question to the network, and the resounding an-
> swer was "Don't do it!" The experience of companies who
> had such facilities advised that it was too expensive, time-
> consuming, and would be a distraction from the core mis-
> sion. The advice was to focus this money on the programs,
> processes, and people, not a building. We took this advice
> and saved an estimated $2 million or more in capital expen-
> ditures alone.[7]

Improving Quality

One of the major benefits of peer-to-peer network membership
is the impact it has on corporate quality. For example, at a recent network meeting, the head of executive development for a
major U.S. bank said that she had been charged with developing a coaching process for the bank. She described the current
coaching process as the "Wild, Wild West of coaching." She
emphasized that no coaching standards, metrics, hiring criteria, or pricing guidelines were currently in place at the bank. In
other words, the bank had an out-of-control process with no
quality management.

In addition, the firm was spending millions on external
coaches, but nobody had any idea who these coaches were or
what value the bank (which was paying for them) was receiving

from the coaching engagements. After the woman recounted this situation to her network peers, two colleagues said that they had been in exactly the same situation very recently. They had each spent the last six months putting together comprehensive coaching processes for their companies—and they would be happy to e-mail their completed plans.

In addition to immediately saving the $100,000 to $200,000 that this information would have cost if the bank's internal resources had been used, this sharing of best practices almost certainly improved the quality of the solution.

Improving Individual Effectiveness and Job Satisfaction

Belonging to a peer-to-peer network benefits members personally and professionally in a number of ways. They develop strong professional relationships and friendships with true peers in other leading companies. These are people with similar problems, opportunities, and challenges. Knowing that you have a group of trusted and objective colleagues you can call on when you need help, advice, and support is like money in the bank: it will keep providing dividends.

Beyond the individual benefit, members and their companies benefit from constantly tapping into what other leading companies are thinking, planning, and doing. As Ray Vigil, vice president and chief learning officer of Humana, noted: "I have found networks to be invaluable to me on a number of occasions, such as conducting best-practices exercises, sharing new and innovative programs, dialoguing with some of the best thought leaders in the field, and gaining valuable input on program design and effectiveness . . . I consider participation as one of my 'must do' activities in my annual personal development and planning."

Advancing the Field

Peer-to-peer networks provide a way of pooling the members' expert intellectual resources to address longer-range challenges of the profession and contribute to the development of their field as a whole. This is collective intelligence at its best.

Peer-to-peer networks hold a great deal of promise for helping organizations adapt to and take advantage of the rapid changes taking place internally within their businesses and externally in their business environment. An increasing number of forward-thinking senior executives say that the ability to network will be an increasingly important skill for leaders in their organizations in the future. They emphasize that developing powerful external networks will be critical to the success of both individual leaders and their enterprises.

These trends suggest that smart investments in improving your networking quotient and improving the size and quality of your networks not only are necessary but will reward you both personally and professionally.

Assess your Peer-to-Peer Networks

1. How many peer-to-peer networks do you belong to?

2. Do your peer-to-peer networks have significant diversity?

3. How often do you consult with your networks?

4. Do you receive information that helps you perform your job better? Do you give useful information to others?

5. Are there ways in which you could improve these networks? For example, do your networks need well-planned meetings, a better Web site, more teleconferences? Can you initiate these changes?

Create or Join a Peer-to-Peer Network Today

Why do you need to be a part of a peer-to-peer network?

➤ *You owe it to yourself.* Peer-to-peer networking is the anti-
dote to professional isolation. We all need to be stimulated
by the best and brightest in our field. A great network provides that stimulation through engagement with true peers
from leading organizations and through exposure to expert
consultants, academics, and breakthrough research. Networks provide a safe harbor—a place to test your thinking
and ideas and ask questions with supportive colleagues who
are there to help and not to judge. Some people have come
to see participation in a peer network as a matter of career
survival and have begun to write network membership into
their employment contract.

➤ *You owe it to your organization.* Why would you want to
reinvent the wheel when you could easily find out how
other leading companies have already solved the same
problem you're facing or created an innovative process or
system similar to what you need? We all have an obligation
to keep abreast of the latest thinking, best practices, innovations, and breakthroughs in our field. Without a doubt, a
well-run community of kindred spirits—peers from top-
notch organizations dedicated to sharing and learning together—is the most efficient and cost-effective way to share
this kind of information.

We are speaking here of *collective intelligence*. This sharing
of intelligence and experience is one of the great strengths of
our human species. From the first sharing of skills, like the use
of fire, humans have employed their collective intelligence to
create our complex civilization. Information technology is now
multiplying this skill sharing exponentially—and peer-to-peer
networks are a key part of this collective movement.

7

Tapping Organizational Networks

If you are well along in your career, are happy with your progress, and see a bright future in the organization where you work, you may think that networking is not important for you professionally. After all, you're advancing at a good pace and don't feel the need to seek out opportunities outside your organization—you know where you're going. You may think the best thing for you would be to keep your head down and focus on your job: if you shine at your job, you'll get the next promotion that much quicker. Spending time networking would just be a distraction. You might think that, but if you do, you could be heading for a tumble.

Why You Need to Tap into Organizational Networks

The fact is that every organization has networks, often hard to spot, that are separate and distinct from those shown on the official organizational chart. The organizational chart shows you who does what and who reports to whom, but it doesn't show you who *talks* to whom, who *knows* what, and how the work *ac-*

tually gets done. Politics also plays a role in the life of every organization and often profoundly affects the decisions that get made—and politics most often flows along networks.

Moreover, with many businesses restructuring to eliminate layers of management and functional silos, what we might call the "network organization" is likely to become a key factor for organizations in the future. We're starting to see the emergence of work outcomes that are driven primarily by loose, informal networks. These networks form to produce a work outcome and then dissolve when that outcome has been achieved.

These networks may stay tightly connected for a year or a few years if the work outcome is complex, or they may disband after a few hours if the work outcome is simple. Research on internal organization networks has ascertained that it is critical for people to have diverse networks within their firms. It's also critical that people understand the dynamics of these networks so that they can manage their access and involvement in an active way.

You need to pay attention to organizational networks as if your career depended on it—because it does. You'll want to develop a keen awareness of how to analyze organizational networks so you can determine which networks are important for you to connect with or be a part of. In order to "see" a network within an organization, you must have a way to identify it, gather information on it, and visualize it. A lot of work on this subject has been done by academics over the years. Some of the best has been done by Rob Cross at the University of Virginia. Much of my thinking about organizational networks has been influenced by Rob, who has written two books that have been extremely important to understanding how networks really form and operate in an organizational context: *Networks in the Knowledge Economy* and *The Hidden Power of Social Networks: Understanding How Work Really Gets Done in Organizations.*

I talked to Rob, he explained why understanding the tional networks around you is so important, especially if your career is advancing and you're reaching the senior levels of your organization:

You need to continually make sure that you're not becoming insular. There's a great tendency in organizations for people to become focused on their own objectives and, as they rise, for people around them to consume more and more of their time. Exactly at points where leaders or others need better connectivity, new insights, innovative thinking, new opportunities, and things that keep them fresh and making good decisions, they're hearing the same voices over and over again. We know that people who fight that tendency off and continue to bridge out even when they don't see the immediate opportunity tend to do much better. Over their career, they're paid more, they're more mobile, and they advance more rapidly. My work shows they're more likely to be in the top 20 percent.

And, Rob said, you need to focus on the network before you really need it: "One of the most common things we find about our high-performer work is that the high performers are much more likely to be out exploring possibilities. It may be a year or two later when suddenly something comes along that they're able to capitalize on because they interacted with somebody a year ago over a potential project. Maybe it was just a lunch conversation that they initiated, but it opens up their ability to capitalize on things because they know and have seeded more of these relationships than people with more limited networks."

Rob argues that networking is especially important in today's flatter, more collaborative organizations, which means you need to spend time not only building networks but analyzing them. A result of these restructuring efforts is that work and collaboration increasingly occur through informal networks of relationships rather than through formal reporting structures as found on an organizational chart or in standard operating procedures. Understanding these invisible networks, he said, has become central to improving performance and strategy execution: "People need some sort of ability to visualize how and where they're spending their time relationally and to continually refine their own connectivity in ways that make them more productive. As collaboration becomes more central to pretty much everything, dynamically visualizing and analyzing one's network is the kind of thing that can free up people's time so they can invest it more productively." He added that his research shows that analyzing the networks within organizations can have a significant impact on performance, learning, and innovation.

Analyzing Organizational Networks

It's clear that the sorts of organizational networks Rob is talking about are not represented by the contents of your Rolodex or BlackBerry—the way your personal network is. To understand how the networks in your organization work, who is in them, and how they overlap (or fail to overlap), you need to conduct what Rob calls Organizational Network Analysis (ONA). ONA involves identifying a strategically important group or process in the organization that could be important to map and then identifying the relationships among the members of the group. What is the information flow—who goes to whom for information? What are the power relationships? Who are the actual decision makers?

According to Rob, this information can be gathered in a variety of ways, from tracking and analyzing e-mails to having researchers observe people for a period of time. Usually the most efficient method is to ask people to complete a survey that has been designed to help map networking relationships. Once the required information has been gathered, you can analyze it using one of several available software packages, most of which produce a variety of network diagrams that represent the network visually, as shown below in figures 7.1 and 7.2. (Describing the full ONA methodology is beyond the scope of this book. Much more information can be gathered at Rob's Web site: http://www.robcross.org.) And if you do all this, what do you get? Rob gives an explanation on his Web site and kindly gave me permission to reprint it here (from http://www.robcross .org/network_ona.htm).

Introduction to Organizational Network Analysis

Organizational network analysis (ONA) can provide an X-ray into the inner workings of an organization—a powerful means of making invisible patterns of information flow and collaboration in strategically important groups visible. For example, we conducted an ONA of executives in the exploration and production division of a large petroleum organization. This group was in the midst of implementing a technology to help transfer knowledge across drilling initiatives and was also interested in assessing their ability as a group to create and share knowledge. As can be seen below, the network analysis revealed a striking contrast between the group's formal and informal structure.

Three important points quickly emerged from the ONA:

First, the ONA identified midlevel managers that were critical in terms of information flow within the group. A particular surprise came from the very central role that Cole played in terms of both overall information flow within the group and being the only point of contact between members of the production division and the rest of the network. If he were hired away, the efficiency of this group as a whole

Figure 7.1 A Network Diagram

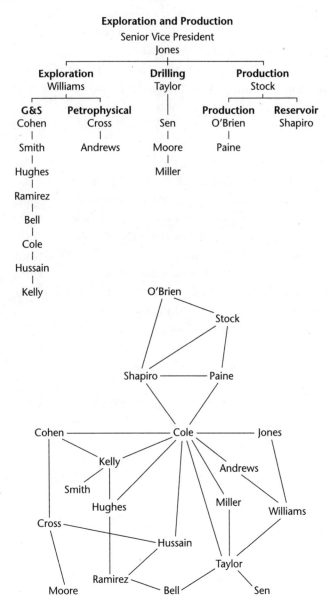

would be significantly impacted while people in the informal network reestablished important informational relationships. Simply categorizing various informational requests that Cole received and then allocating ownership of these informational or decision domains to other executives served to both unburden Cole and make the overall network more responsive and robust.

Second, the ONA helped to identify highly peripheral people that essentially represented untapped expertise and underutilized resources for the group. In particular, it became apparent that many of the senior people had become too removed from the day-to-day operations of this group. For example, the most senior person (Jones) was one of the most peripheral in the informal network. This is a common finding. As people move higher within an organization, their work begins to entail more administrative tasks, which makes them both less accessible and less knowledgeable about the day-to-day work of their subordinates. Indeed, in this case, our debrief session indicated that Jones had become too removed and his lack of responsiveness frequently held the entire network back when important decisions needed to be made.

Third, the ONA also demonstrated the extent to which the production division (the subgroup on the top of the diagram) had become separated from the overall network. Several months prior to this analysis these people had been physically moved to a different floor in the building. Upon reviewing the network diagram, many of the executives realized that this physical separation had resulted in loss of a lot of the serendipitous meetings that occurred when they were co-located. Structured meetings were set up to help avoid operational problems the group had been experiencing due to this loss of communication between production and the rest of the network.

This simple vignette provides a quick overview regarding how ONA can be applied to important departments or functions within organizations. However, many strategically important networks do not reside on the formal organization chart. ONA can be used to address various organizational issues:

1. Supporting partnerships and alliances
2. Assessing strategy execution
3. Improving strategic decision making in top leadership networks
4. Integrating networks across core processes
5. Promoting innovation
6. Ensuring integration post-merger or large-scale change
7. Developing communities of practice
8. Personal networks and leadership development

Interpreting a Network Diagram

Information collected from social network surveys can be used to create network diagrams that illustrate the relationships between members of a group. The network below reveals information flow within a dispersed new product development team. In this case each member of the team was asked, "Whom do you turn to for information to get your work done?" The network has been color-coded to differentiate between team members that are in manufacturing, finance, and marketing.

Lines and Arrows. The diagram above shows the flow of information within a new-product development team. Each line indicates an information link between two people; arrows represent the direction of the relationship (incoming arrows show that the person is a source of information; outgoing arrows show that the team member seeks information from the linked parties).

Figure 7.2 Interpreting a Network Diagram

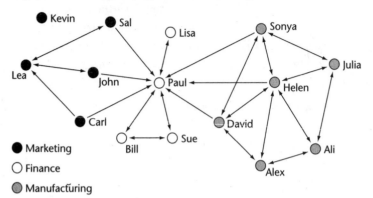

Central People. Network diagrams make clear who the most prominent people within a group are. On this team, nine people rely on Paul for information. Not only do his colleagues in finance come to him, but also people in marketing and manufacturing. Paul himself does not reach out to people outside of finance.

The diagram alone can't tell us if Paul's impact is positive or negative. If the group is overly dependent on him, he may be a bottleneck, slowing the flow of information and holding up decisions. On the other hand, people like Paul often play a very positive role, providing valuable information and holding a group together.

Peripheral People. Some people are only loosely connected to a network; a few may be completely isolated—members in theory but not in practice. In this network, no one goes to Carl for information, and Kevin is out of the loop entirely. As is true with central people, the diagram alone doesn't say anything about the value of peripheral people.

Sometimes, such outsiders turn out to be underutilized resources, and integrating them can be critical to a network's effectiveness and efficiency. Other times, people are peripheral for good reason. Perhaps they are trying to manage work-family balance or are specialists such as research scientists, who need to maintain strong ties to academia. And, on occasion, people are peripheral because they lack skills, social and otherwise, for the job.

Subgroups. Groups within a network often arise as a product of location, function, hierarchy, tenure, age, or gender. In this case, the team is split by function; very little information is being shared among the three groups. Moreover, connections in marketing and finance are sparse, while the manufacturing subgroup is tightly knit. That can be good or bad. It may be that the manufacturing people have developed communication practices that the team as a whole could use to its benefit. It's also possible that those people rely on one another so heavily that they are preventing integration. Again, only follow-up interviews can reveal which scenario is true.

All this might seem quite complicated—but in today's large, complex organizations with hundreds of millions of dollars riding on effective teamwork and decision making, the investment in ONA is very worthwhile. "At a specific leader level, ONA provides an X-ray into how things are actually working," Rob told me. The problem is that every leader walks around with a picture in his or her head of how the organization is being run, which may or may not be accurate. "Whether it's a division, a team, or a full organization, ONA provides leaders with a more accurate view of where things are going well and where they're not—and this enables leaders to take action in very different ways than by merely manipulating the formal organizational structure," Rob said.

"I think it's very central for a leader to understand connectivity to her own network," he added, "and how it's working because it plays such a huge role in how she learns, how she makes decisions, how she gets information to consider new opportunities or restructurings. Leaders need to understand that certain biases creep into the information that is presented to them. Knowing that you're listening to the right people is a really big strategic imperative at that level." Understanding the network around you therefore allows you to see where biases may be coming from and how to correct them.

Organizational Networks and Leadership Development

Rob has also focused heavily on how networking affects leadership development. We've already briefly discussed some of his work on how top performers (the top 20 percent) use networks more effectively than more typical managers. It makes sense, therefore, for organizations to provide their managers and executives with the tools and resources that will help them build their networking skills and to help them build networks that are actually useful, not just large. It also makes sense to assess the networking factors that contribute to a leader's effectiveness. Rob's research shows that managers and executives should pay attention to six factors: hierarchical balance, bridging relationships, structured versus unstructured relationships, time invested, physical proximity, and replenishment rate. (I have changed some of Rob's terminology to make it clearer for the nonspecialist.) Let's look at each of these critical factors for organizational networking.

- ► *Hierarchical balance.* While peer-to-peer networks provide safe learning environments precisely because they are composed of your peers, this is not an advantage for your organizational networks. You need to manage relationships with those higher than, at the same levels, and lower than you, which creates a hierarchical balance Rob calls "a hallmark of a well-rounded organizational network." Networking only with your organizational peers may give you a myopic view of what is happening. You may lose the front-line perspective of those in lower ranks and the more strategic insight to be gained from those higher in the organization.

► *Bridging relationships.* New employees usually focus on and learn from people in their own department. But as you gain experience and take on more responsibility, it becomes important to form relationships that bridge to other departments and organizations. Unfortunately, people often wait too long to build bridging relationships. "A common example of this is the leader who's rising in the organization and continuing to hold tightly to 70 or 80 percent of his network in the function that he came from," Rob said. "At exactly the point that he needs to diversify to be effective, he allows a certain sphere to overly influence his thinking and decision making, and it becomes a problem."

► *Structured versus unstructured relationships.* Many managers are so tightly scheduled that their calendars are packed with back-to-back meetings all day long, every workday. This may indicate that you are locked into a routine that may not bring you the information you need. Are you connecting with the people you really need to build relationships with or simply with those who make it on your schedule because of organizational routines and emergencies?

► *Time invested in maintaining the right relationships.* Many people spend a lot of time and effort in the upkeep of relationships that are well established and need little additional investment or in those that offer little benefit. They invest their time in networking but not as productively as they could because they don't seek out the right relationships.

- *Physical proximity.* The probability of networking with someone decreases as you get farther away. With senior leaders, this can result in not understanding the problems, goals, and needs of people in different locations, such as regional offices.

- *Replenishment rate.* Do you work on renewing your organizational network, or does it tend to remain static? If your network this year is the same as last year's, you are probably not learning new things from your network. On the other hand, if you have a lot of turnover in your network, you may not be working to maintain established relationships with mentors or confidants who know you well—people to whom you can take personal or difficult issues. Your organizational network should be refreshed regularly but still maintain continuity. You need a mix of old and new.

Looking at each of these six factors can help you improve your organizational networks, according to Rob—and greatly strengthen your leadership development: "What we're able to show people through the high-performer research and then through the ONA software is how they look in these dimensions, how they stack up against other peer groups, and where they might be falling into traps by not paying attention to their connectivity."

Do You Want to Be Among the Top Performers?

As we have seen, networking is not just for those who are looking for a job, seeking to change careers, or trying to find opportunities as independent business owners or consultants. Even if you work in a large organization and are happy with your career there, you must make networking a priority. And while your organizational network will no doubt overlap with your personal network, you should see it as distinct and consider the role it plays in your career. If you want to be among the top performers of your organization, remember what Rob told me about managers who invest in their organizational networks and constantly keep them refreshed: "Over their careers, they're paid more, they're more mobile, and they advance more rapidly."

In the next chapter, we'll discuss an important form of networking: communities of practice—communities based on common interests or concerns.

8

Joining Communities of Practice

In 1999, the state of Pennsylvania decided to work more intentionally across agencies to address the issue of transitioning children with disabilities from school to work. Rather than creating a "department of transition," the state convened a community of practice that brought together practitioners involved in transition issues from all the different agencies and departments concerned. By forming a community, these practitioners remained with their agencies, doing the work they did there, but they brought their perspectives together, collaborated across agency silos, and learned with one another. They also started to organize annual conferences to bring together practitioners from across the state who had local "transition councils," including educators, government workers, and businesspeople, as well as parents.

At the third annual conference in 2004, interagency teams from five other states were invited to visit and learn from the Pennsylvania experience. To this day, the state representatives meet regularly, on the phone and face-to-face, as the national Interagency Transition Community of Practice. This creates a system of heterogeneous communities of practice at various levels of scale, from the local councils to the various inter-agency communities in the participating states to the national community of state representatives. The project is part of the IDEA (Individuals with Disabilities Education Act) Partner-ship, which has a grant from the Education Department to support national communities of practice on various topics re-lated to special education.

"Communities of practice are groups of people who share a concern, a set of problems, or a passion about a topic and who deepen their knowledge and expertise in this area by interact-ing on an ongoing basis," according to Etienne Wenger, one of the leading authorities on CoPs and coauthor of *Cultivating Communities of Practice: A Guide to Managing Knowledge*.

When I interviewed Etienne, he told me a community of practice has three core components: domain, community, and practice:

➤ The *domain* is the area of shared inquiry and the key issues a community of practice explores, such as childhood health, automotive engineering, or the welfare of a regional park. Because of their common interest in a domain, mem-bers of the CoP have a shared competence, even if they come from different disciplines. For example, a doctor and a teacher who are members of a CoP network whose do-main is childhood health will have overlapping expertise on that topic.

A **community of practice** is a group of people who join to-gether to help each other solve problems and develop knowl-edge and expertise in an area of shared interest.

➤ A CoP is a *community* of people, not just a collection of individuals, because they engage in joint activities and discussions, share information, and help each other. They build relationships that enable them to learn from each other and have a sense of belonging to the CoP. In the case of the childhood health CoP, the doctor and teacher will join with others in the CoP to share stories, solve problems, find resources, advocate for their domain, and help each other.

➤ A community of *practice* goes beyond having a shared interest to actually taking steps to learn, solve problems, and advance understanding. Members of a CoP develop a shared inventory of experiences, stories, methods, and ways of addressing problems, a shared practice. In the example of the childhood health CoP, members do not merely have an academic interest in studying children's health but actually take action to advance childhood health.

These three elements make CoPs a unique form of network. They share some characteristics with other kinds of networks but have distinctive features all their own (see table 8.1). Communities of practice are different from work groups or project teams. A community of practice may exist within an organization, but many communities of practice are composed of people who do not work together and who may never meet face-to-face. Membership in most communities of practice is voluntary, but some employers require or strongly encourage participation among their employees.

In communities of practice with voluntary membership, members are self-selected by their interest in the issue that is the focus of the community. If interest in the issue declines and the community is no longer active, the members may choose to disband.

Table 8.1 Distinctions Between Communities of Practice and Other Structures

Type of network	Purpose	Who belongs?	How clear are the boundaries?	What holds them together?	How long do they last?
Community of practice	To create, expand, and exchange knowledge and to develop individual capabilities	Self-selection of individuals based on expertise or passion for a topic	Fuzzy	Passion for, commitment to, and identification with the group and its expertise	Evolve and end organically (last as long as there is relevance to the topic and value and interest in learning together)
Formal department	To deliver a product or service	Everyone who reports to the group's manager	Clear	Job requirements and common goals	Are intended to be ongoing (but last until the next reorganization)
Operational team	To take care of an ongoing operation or process	Members assigned by management	Clear	Shared responsibility for the operation	Are intended to be ongoing (but last as long as the operation is needed)
Project team	To accomplish a specified task	People who have a direct role in accomplishing the task	Clear	The project's goals and milestones	Have a predetermined ending (when the project is completed)
Community of interest	To be informed	Whoever is interested	Fuzzy	Access to the information and sense of like-mindedness	Evolve and end organically
Informal network	To receive and pass on information, to know who is who	Friends and business acquaintances	Undefined	Mutual needs and relationships	Never really start or end (exist as long as people keep in touch or remember each other)

Contributions of Communities of Practice

Although the name is new, communities of practice have been around since the dawn of civilization. If you think about it, you may realize that you already belong to one or more CoPs if you bring a level of expertise to an area and share your insights and knowledge with others who are also involved in the area.

A number of factors make CoP networks useful and important. Through a CoP framework, professional networks focus on providing short- and long-term value to both the members and the organizations in which they work. In the short term, members gain help with challenges, access to expertise, and confidence; accomplish meaningful work; and have fun with colleagues.

In the long term, members gain personal development, professional identity, a stronger personal network, and an enhanced reputation and marketability. Organizations benefit in the short term from problem solving, time saving, knowledge sharing, and synergistic interactions with other organizations. In the long term, organizations increase their strategic capabilities and innovation and keep abreast of important trends.

Shared passion across a domain is becoming a necessity in our era of unprecedented change. I believe that the challenges of this new century can be addressed only through effective use of our collective intelligence. CoP networks provide a unique tool to leverage this collective intelligence, which is, to me, probably the most important reason to understand them better. As Etienne told me, what is so special about CoPs is that "the community itself acts as a living knowledge asset." He pointed out (as Rob Cross did in the previous chapter) that early efforts at managing knowledge focused on information systems and databases—and yielded disappointing results. CoPs offer a new approach, he says, which focuses on people and on the social structures that enable them to learn with and from each other.

Communities of Practice as a Knowledge Management Tool

Businesses are turning to CoP networks because they realize that knowledge is a critical asset that needs to be managed strategically—and that CoP networks can provide a powerful tool in that regard. Etienne said, "Many companies today establish communities of practice as a way to manage their knowledge assets, and part of that strategy is the development of people. A community of practice does not distinguish between developing people and developing knowledge assets because the community itself acts as a living knowledge asset." He cited Chrysler as an example of a company that has set up CoPs for its staff: "Chrysler has various car platforms (small cars, big cars, and minivans), and they've established communities of practice that cut across those areas for designers who design similar parts. In many ways, the design of brakes for the minivan is different from that of a small car, but they are similar enough that CoPs are a good mechanism for joint learning." Engineers across Chrysler who worked on windshield wipers, believe it or not, also formed a CoP.

The resources to meet the tremendous challenges we face in the twenty-first century lie in our collective intelligence (knowledge and wisdom). CoPs are designed to gather and disseminate this collective intelligence through meetings (face-to-face or virtual), online peer networking, teleconferences, research, Web sites, blogs, wikis, and other appropriate tools. CoPs achieve personal, professional, and organizational effectiveness, that is, produce a return on investment (ROI) by

► Solving pressing problems
► Saving money and better using resources
► Saving time
► Enhancing members' standing in their professions and organizations
► Improving the quality of decisions
► Developing personal capabilities and frameworks
► Accelerating innovation and advancing the field

CoPs are designed to tap multiple dimensions of members' collective intelligence. CoPs emphasize a blend of intellectual, emotional, and social intelligence and design network experiences to address objectives in each of these areas. CoP members support each other by

► Teaching and learning from one another
► Being responsive to requests from one another
► Being forthcoming with advice and guidance
► Actively participating in meetings, surveys, teleconferences, and online peer networking
► Openly sharing information and best practices
► Providing career guidance (coaching and mentoring) and support to one another

Intellectual intelligence is catalyzed by addressing relevant content topics and issues with leading thought experts, drawing on the areas of expertise of each network member, and bringing these to bear on "hot buttons" being faced by members in their work.

In a CoP framework, the exchange of intellectual intelligence is optimized when individuals are aware of what they are feeling and why they are feeling it and are able to manage those feelings. This emotional intelligence goes hand in hand with empathy for others and the social skills to communicate these feelings, namely, social intelligence. Successful CoPs create powerful connections that provide

- Deeper understanding (personally and professionally)
- Long-term relationships that transcend a rapidly changing business environment
- Personal friendships
- Quick, quality, timely help
- Encouragement and support

A core tenet of CoPs is that everyone has something to teach and everyone has something to learn; thus, interactions among members are designed to leverage the participants' knowledge and experience by using icebreakers, team building, and fun to bring members into intimate and valued relationships with one another. The commitment to establishing deep, trusted connections is at the heart of every CoP and drives a rich culture that members work to evolve and develop. CoPs provide high value for time by

- Responding quickly to requests for help
- Having great meetings (in person or virtual)
- Having quick access to people, ideas, and knowledge and not having to reinvent the wheel
- Facilitating collaboration between members
- Helping members solve critical challenges

Keys to Effective Communities of Practice

Because of their distinctive nature, CoP networks need a different approach to thrive. While organizational or personal networks can be managed informally, CoPs need someone specifically designated to maintain them. When I asked Etienne whether CoP networks could run themselves without an active facilitator, he replied emphatically, "It's not possible!" He continued:

> As a matter of fact, having a facilitator is one of the key success factors found for communities of practice. Some people use the term "facilitators," others say "coordinator" or "leader," but you need someone who cares about the community. Two main things that make a community of practice a success are high value for time invested and someone who keeps the community engaged. You need someone who will make sure that whenever people engage, they are getting value for the time they're spending to participate. You also need to recognize that people have all kinds of demands on their time, and the community may fall apart unless there is someone who cares enough to bring it back to the attention of the members.

In other words, a CoP network thrives only when at least one person is actively making sure that it is vibrant and offers a useful learning experience to the members. If you are a member of a CoP that seems rudderless and find it of value, you should consider jumping in to facilitate interactions or it might dissolve before your eyes.

Leading a CoP Network

Leaders or facilitators of CoP networks need a number of competencies, Etienne told me. "For a community leader, the most important competency is networking. Successful leaders keep in touch with the community and can sense where the community is going because they are in touch with the people." All the skills and behaviors I discussed in the first part of the book come into play here. Successful leaders listen as much as they talk and place the concerns of others on a par with their own. "The ability to give people a voice through the community is a critical competency," he said.

Leaders of a CoP also need to help the community advocate for its domain. Because the members are practitioners, their work needs to be valued in the larger organization or in society as a whole. The CoP needs to be able to attract resources of many kinds—people, money, support materials, meeting places, and so on. All that takes advocacy, whether it is for childhood health, regional parks, or windshield wiper technology, to use the examples we have previously discussed.

"Another key competency," Etienne told me, "is the ability to help people make a contribution and take leadership in an area. You have to let a community find its voice, let the members find their voice and their identities as community contributors." Every organization is stronger when it has many people assuming leadership roles in one way or another, and that certainly applies to CoP networks.

At the level of practice, a key competency is collective trust. "Every member should be able to bring a problem they have to the community and in turn have the community try to help. People shouldn't have to position themselves constantly. They should be able to talk about their problems as they see them." This, Etienne says, is a key component of a good community: the ability to expose a problem and engage with it. Sweeping problems under the rug damages collective trust.

Other competencies include strong communication skills and the ability to produce good documents, such as minutes of meetings, position papers, and the like, so that members can easily reconnect when they leave a meeting.

Communities of practice are increasingly moving online. We look at how the Internet is changing networking in the next chapter.

► For More Insight

This has been a brief look at communities of practice. For much more insight, I encourage you to read Etienne Wenger's book, mentioned earlier. Much of this chapter is drawn from the work of Etienne Wenger, but the views presented here are my own and represent only my interpretation of his work and—aside from direct quotes—should not be ascribed to him.

9

Virtual
Networking

Virtual networking is the new frontier. In 2006, *Time* magazine's Person of the Year was not the usual politician or philanthropist. Instead, the cover simply read, "You. Yes, you. You control the Information Age. Welcome to your world."[8] The premise was that individual user-generated content is growing dramatically and rapidly influencing society. People have begun turning to the Internet for a great deal of their regular activities, including social interaction on a number of levels.

In this chapter, we'll take a brief look at this phenomenon and then discuss how you can take advantage of it. The virtual Connect Effect can put you in touch with any number of people who share interests similar to yours. We'll also discuss virtual etiquette—the dos and don'ts of social networking.

My definition of virtual networking is any networking that is done with people you have never met face-to-face or the act of networking using interactions that are not face-to-face. This means that this form of networking could be done via mail, telephone, or fax. In actuality, these days, it's done mainly over the Internet.

The great benefit of virtual networking is the ease with which you can connect to people anytime, anywhere. This can be done asynchronously (that is, without being connected to someone in real time, such as by e-mail) or synchronously (connected in real time via instant messaging [IM] or a video teleconference). And with cell phones' increasing access to the Web, you don't even need to be at your computer to network online. In fact, Coca-Cola recently announced that it is creating a network specifically designed for mobile phones under its Sprite brand where members can set up profiles, post pictures, and make new friends.

With an online network, you can connect one to one or one to a few or as a group. Even large groups can interact asynchronously, such as via a wiki or threaded discussion or through companies like Instancy. (If these words are unfamiliar to you, see "A Few Definitions.") They can also interact synchronously, using technologies that are available today such as Live Meeting, WebEx, Centra Software, and I-Cohere, for example. Services like Skype have even brought the telephone to the Internet.

Virtual networking can take any number of different forms. Various sites are dedicated to file and video sharing, online encyclopedia/knowledge databases, auctions, and classified ads to name a few, but at present, virtual networking tends to be dominated by social networking sites, such as MySpace (http://www.myspace.com), which have become all-inclusive portals of networking data and communication. Even large online portals such as those of Microsoft and Yahoo! have formed their own virtual networking platforms, Windows Live Spaces and Yahoo! 360°, because of the potential this new type of environment holds in attracting a large online audience. Indeed, it is a safe bet that virtual networking will continue to increase its dominance in the way that people interact via the Internet.

(And with the speed at which the Internet changes, please forgive me if some of this material is out of date by the time you read this!)

The Evolution of Online Networking

Initially, at least within the United States, before the World Wide Web even took off, major American Internet providers (such as America Online, CompuServe, and Prodigy) essentially had online networking, but it was restricted to members of the same service provider. Simple e-mail was transferred

---

A Few Definitions

A **wiki** is a Web site or page on a site that allows visitors to add, remove, and edit material. Wikipedia, an online encyclopedia, is one of the best known wikis.

A **blog** (short for web log) is like an online diary on a particular subject, such as food, politics, or industry news, where entries are written in chronological order, with the newest entry on top. Most blogs allow readers to post comments to individual items.

A **discussion forum** allows people to communicate about common interests asynchronously, in their own time and at their own pace. An individual may post a message in the evening and another may respond the next day.

A **threaded discussion** is an electronic discussion in which messages are grouped visually in a hierarchy by topic. A set of messages on a single topic is called a "topic thread" or simply "thread."

into chat rooms and chat rooms into instant messaging (a real-time, "private chat room" that allows communication between two individuals). When the World Wide Web came about in 1993, contact among all providers from throughout the world became a reality. The revolutionary decision to make the World Wide Web free ensured that the Internet would be able to grow and reach an incredible number of individuals. Instant messaging became increasingly popular, and programs such as AIM (an offshoot of AOL's internal Instant Messenger service), ICQ, Yahoo! Messenger, and MSN (Hotmail) Messenger bridged the gap among all.

Still, even as instant messaging programs became increasingly prominent, contact was generally restricted to those who knew one another beforehand, either directly or through an intermediary, and to those who happened to find one another through a specifically themed chat room (Singles in Detroit or Star Wars Fans, for example). Personal blogs then began to show up throughout the Internet, as people chronicled their daily activities or thoughts. One of the first such sites was Live-Journal.com. According to the site, it has over 10 million active members, who can grant access to their blogs to the general public or to whomever they please.

These personal blogs eventually evolved into more subject-oriented forums where the focus became not the meanderings of an individual or group of individuals but discussion and interaction around particular subjects of interest. It is natural for us to appeal to colleagues or experts in a field when we have specific questions or issues that we want to discuss; the Internet has also allowed for this by way of discussion forums (similar to a blog but involving discussion and contributions from a number of individuals), a concept that has been applied to personal, professional, and even academic settings.

We're also seeing networking support tools start to be available on the Internet. Services like LinkedIn provide an environment where users can tap into the networks of friends and colleagues.

The firm Visible Path is using search algorithms to map a user's network (by searching Outlook files, for example), calculate the strength of relationships within this network, and then connect the networks of friends and colleagues together in a six-degrees-of-separation-type of environment.

More and more of these tools will become available, and they will make it much easier for all of us to build, maintain, and leverage our networks, whether our networks are personal, professional, or virtual.

A word of caution is in order, though. Even though they are online and may have lots of bells and whistles, networking Web sites, like all networks, are only as interesting and useful as the people in them—and you get out of them only what you put in them. Don't expect to sign up on an online network, click a few links here and there, and make dozens of new friends or business contacts. Even in the virtual world, there is no such thing as a free lunch. To get the most out of a virtual network, expect to put in as much time and effort as you do for your offline, face-to-face networks.

Virtual networking can be business oriented or it can be purely social. In this chapter, we're going to look at both social networking and professional networking.

Social Networking

The popularity of social networking has grown exponentially over the last few years. The best example is MySpace (http://www.myspace.com), which, the company claims, has more than 100 million users and a growth rate of 250,000 a day!

The early adopters of virtual networking are certainly younger adults—the Millenniums, Gen Ys and Gen Xers—but that doesn't mean that older generations will not jump on the bandwagon as more sites appear that are targeted at their particular needs and interests.

Bringing people with preexisting connections online is where the concept of online social networks originated. The Internet would allow these networks to come back together, to evolve, and to grow in ways they otherwise would not have been able to. In 1995 this idea was put into practice by Randy Conrads, who wanted to use the Internet to bring people with common backgrounds together. Classmates (http://www.classmates .com)—according to Wikipedia, the first social networking Web site—was founded with the intention of putting former high school friends and colleagues back into contact with one another and is credited with making online social networking mainstream. Access to the Web site is free, and the Web site remains profitable thanks to online advertising. With over 40 million members, Classmates has evolved into a site that lets people network based on common elementary schools, high schools, colleges, or places of employment and has even allowed a number of people to find lost loves and family members.

The popularity of these sites rapidly grew and spawned an international profusion of social networking sites, such as Bebo (http://www.bebo.com), which is very successful in Britain, with around 34 million members, and Orkut (http://www.orkut.com), a Google-owned site that is popular in Brazil, with 46 million people on board. Other social networks include Xanga (http://www.xanga.com), Friendster (http://www.friendster .com), and Facebook (http://www.facebook.com).

In these online networks, an initial set of founders sends out messages inviting members of their own personal networks to join the site. New members repeat the process, growing the total number of members and links in the network. Sites offer features such as automatic address book updates, viewable profiles, the ability to form new links through "introduction services," and other forms of online social connections. Let's take a look at a couple of phenomenally successful social networking sites.

MySpace

As I write this, MySpace seems to be the most popular social networking site (of course, something else may have superseded it by the time you read this). It advertises itself as a "lifestyle portal for connecting with friends, discovering popular culture, and making a positive impact on the world" and claims more than 100 million member profiles worldwide. MySpace offers members ways to interact through personal web profiles, blogs, instant messaging, e-mail, music streaming, music videos, photo galleries, classified listings, events, groups, college communities, and member forums and is very popular with teenagers and young adults. MySpace's international network includes localized community sites in the United States, the United Kingdom, Japan, France, Germany, Australia, Ireland, Spain, Italy, Mexico, Canada, the Netherlands, New Zealand, and Latin America.

MySpace essentially allows individuals to make themselves known all across the world via everything from sharing pictures (improving upon the idea of photo-sharing Web sites like Flickr [http://www.flickr.com]) to listing whatever they want about themselves, such as place of residence, place of employment, educational background, and music tastes, just to name a few topics. Users can also see whom other people are friends with and can even communicate using a MySpace internal comment system. People can even integrate songs and videos into their profiles, and they can join specific networking groups (such as Starbucks Baristas or University of California at Los Angeles Nepalese Students) and click to see who else is in them.

The Web site has become so popular that in early 2006, MySpace Mobile was created when Helio, an American cell phone provider, created special cell phones geared toward allowing individuals to access MySpace portably. Currently there are plans to expand MySpace's mobile network. As MySpace's popularity continues to grow, its potential and its position as the Internet's leading social networking site will become larger than ever before. In July 2005, Rupert Murdoch's News Corporation purchased the Web site for $580 million. According to today's estimates, that price was a bargain, to say the least. To put that number into context, on August 8, 2006, the search engine Google signed a $900 million deal just to provide Google search and advertising services on MySpace.

MySpace has turned out to be an extremely powerful (and free) marketing platform. Many aspiring (and even more pop-

---

Politicians Discover Online Networking

Social networking online is a happening thing. And now even politicians are discovering their power to connect with people—and many are putting up profiles on MySpace and other social networking sites. According to TechPresident (http://www.techpresident.com), a political blog that covers how the 2008 presidential candidates are using the Web, Senators Hillary Clinton and Barack Obama have the most "friends" on both MySpace and Facebook. Senator Obama leads with 97,847 MySpace friends and 88,706 Facebook supporters, while Senator Clinton has 88,492 supporters on MySpace and 21,477 on Facebook (as of June 2007). Among the Republican candidates, Senator John McCain leads with 35,867 MySpace friends and 9,197 Facebook friends.

ular) artists and musicians have turned to MySpace to feature their music and promote themselves because of the free potential mass exposure that they could receive. Even politicians are getting into the act. See "Politicians Discover Online Networking."

Facebook

Another very popular social networking platform is Facebook. Facebook was founded as an online version of paper-copy facebooks, which many smaller colleges pass out to incoming freshmen at orientation. The idea of a hard-copy facebook is to be able to see pictures of whom you are going to be spending your next four years in school with along with a little bit of background information about them (where they're from, where they went to high school, what their interests are, etc.). A Harvard student by the name of Mark Zuckerburg saw the potential in bringing this concept online. When the Facebook Web site was started in 2004, it was open exclusively to Harvard students. It was then expanded to the entire Ivy League, followed by a number of other prestigious institutions, and finally to all colleges and universities nationwide. As of December 2005, Facebook had over 7.5 million U.S. college student accounts, and 20,000 were said to be created daily.

Facebook is a social networking site that works in much the same way as MySpace: members can create profile pages, form networks with their friends, send messages, and share photographs. Facebook was originally intended for college students and required that users have a valid academic e-mail address to register. Facebook soon expanded to allow high school pupils to join, and in 2006, it opened its doors to everyone, as its original members graduated. It currently has about 24 million registered users, more than half of whom are not students.

Facebook in particular (although it has been reported on other Web sites as well) has been repetitively targeted by job recruiters. Initially using their old university e-mail addresses, alums have been able to gain access to current students' postings and get to know job applicants beyond their résumés and interviews. Students post pictures of themselves (often partying and the like), or friends "tag" pictures of other users, and if a student is shown to be making decisions that a prospective employer finds to be inappropriate, the student may not be hired as a result. A number of universities, including the University of Michigan and New York University, have even sent out e-mails warning students of this danger.

Social Networking Sites Continue to Multiply

The newest social networks on the Internet are becoming more focused on niches such as art, tennis, football (soccer), golf, cars, dog owners, and even cosmetic surgery. Most of the social networks on the Internet are public, allowing anyone to join. But some are invitation-only.

Hundreds of social networking sites have started to appear on lists or web logs (blogs). When you Google "social networking," you get over 100 million links. When you Google "social networks," you get over 150 million links. Even Microsoft is getting into the game, announcing the launch of Aggreg8— "social network for IT Pros." How can you find social networks beyond the megasites discussed here that match your interests? Resource B provides a few ideas to get you started.

Professional Online Networks

Fast Company, the preeminent "new economy" business magazine of the 1990s, created the online network Company of Friends, introducing business networking to the Internet in

1997. Today, there are hundreds of professionally oriented on-line networking sites, such as career-oriented sites, knowledge-exchange platforms, bulletin boards, and online communities of practice. Some of these are proprietary, set up by a company exclusively for its own employees. Others are independent, open to the general public.

Both internally and externally, companies have found benefits in bringing people together online. Within a firm, the concept of an internal best-practices forum is a relatively inexpensive way to bridge the gap and bring together individuals who would not otherwise be able to network so they can benefit from contact with one another. IBM, for example, has adopted Sametime, an internal chat system that allows employees to contact other IBM employees based on their position, experience, and office location to instantly get answers to their questions and concerns. It also allows limited access to information and lets individuals throughout a large corporation document and comment on specific corporate information, which can be shared with relevant colleagues and parties. Another form of networking is known as "enterprise relationship management" (ERM). Companies install ERM on their own servers and enable employees to share their networks of contacts and relationships to outside people and companies.

Externally, knowledge exchange Web sites have become prominent (and some have evolved into online communities of practice). This trend started in large part within the military and has spread more and more to the corporate world. While a number of internal corporate systems exist, as previously mentioned, several organizations like the Corporate Executive Board offer a virtual service that facilitates best-practices exchange across organizations. Some communities are more general, while some are geared toward specific profiles like executives in charge of corporate learning and development.

Typical Features of Business-Oriented Web Sites

As you can see, business-oriented networking sites are prolifer-
ating rapidly. To understand a bit more about how these sites
work, let's take a deeper dive into one professional networking
site, ITtoolbox (http://www.ittoolbox.com). ITtoolbox is a professional community where peers share knowledge about information technology (IT).

ITtoolbox offers an interactive series of references/forums
in which members are able to discuss hot issues and get answers to their IT questions. The site features over 700 targeted
discussion communities and a million pages of community-
generated content (the number of pages is constantly growing)
and has over 200,000 active members.

The site is organized by groups (i.e., communities), blogs,
wikis, knowledge bases, and professional networking. The
groups section features IT questions and answers among
peers. These are sorted by topic and by type; one can join a
forum through a pop-up window that asks if you are interested
in joining.

The groups are organized into several different types, such
as those focusing on strategy and planning groups, technical
and functional areas, career paths, and information about vendors. Each forum features a summary line, the number of
members in the forum, the number of posts per day, and the
date of origin, in addition to a hot link to a corresponding wiki
section (where members can introduce concepts written in the
forum on the wiki pages).

The blogs section is described as "IT news and knowledge
from the front line." Blogs are sorted based on recent entries,
comments, popular entries and blogs, and IT subjects. The wiki
section features discussion groups, "top contributors [to wikis]
from the past week," and an IT reference guide. It features FAQs

(frequently asked questions), a how-to section, and a code section (source code along with a description of what it does).

The knowledge bases, blogs, and wikis are all bundled by specific topics. The professional networking section has tools that allow professionals to create their own home pages, connect with other professionals, and communicate with the IT community in a productive environment. ITtoolbox does not charge a membership fee but makes its money from advertising.

The Connect Effect Online

LinkedIn (http://www.linkedin.com) is a professional networking service and forum that has proven incredibly successful. The site has been dubbed "MySpace for grown-ups," steering clear of the youthful razzle-dazzle found on that site and zeroing in on helping professionals connect with each other. LinkedIn has truly brought the concept of connections to the virtual stage. In fact, when the site was founded in 2003, the only way to become a member of the Web site was to receive a direct referral. As of June 2007, the company claimed more than 11 million registered users. Unlike most other social networking sites, LinkedIn charges money for a number of its advanced services, but it also makes advertising revenue.

The general premise of the Web site is to establish and gain access to your direct network (your ties), the connections of your ties, and finally the connections of your ties' connections. So by being able to view the profiles of people linked to you by as much as three links, you have the potential of getting in touch with a number of other people by way of a referral. If everybody in the chain approves of a "contact," so to speak, two individuals can be put in touch with one another and a recommendation can be made. It should be noted, however, that anybody in the chain can deny the referral.

Employers can list jobs on the site and search for candidates while candidates for jobs can find HR members at a particular company and establish connections. When people practice the all-important concept of reciprocity, they can help one another when they see potential mutual benefit so that individuals can make sure good candidates get to the right people. Individuals are able to build their reputations through effective matches, for example, and the ability to assess whether two people shall be put together is a kind of efficacy in and of itself. Research has long indicated that great benefits lie behind weak ties/connections, and LinkedIn has managed to capitalize on the wide reach of weak ties as well as rely on the high trust of directly linked strong ties. It should come as no surprise that LinkedIn utilizes its own internal system for job posts and hiring for its own company.

Virtual Networking Dos and Don'ts

Virtual networking is not free of risks. In July 2006, a MySpace ad was hacked and over a million users were hit with a spyware program, which could potentially extract personal information (like credit card numbers) from people's computers without their being aware of it. Of course, there is always the worry that dangerous people will portray themselves as somebody they are not and wreak physical or emotional harm upon others; while virtual networking sites should take some precautionary measures, it is ultimately up to each user to be smart and alert. Whether you network for social reasons, business reasons, or both, you should follow some basic dos and don'ts.

Virtual Networking Dos

► Do *"test drive" organized networks (social, professional, issue or interest specific, etc.) before jumping in with both feet.* Consider restricting access to your page to a select group of people—for example, your friends from school, your club, your team, your community groups, or your family.

► Do *determine as soon as possible what role you'd like to play when you join a preexisting network.* Will you be an active participant, an organizer, a gatekeeper, a lurker (someone who stays on the sidelines and just views what is going on), or a combination of these roles?

► Do *post only information that you are comfortable with others seeing—and knowing—about you.* Many people can see your page, including your parents, your teachers, the police, or the company you might want to work for in five years.

► Do *practice reciprocity.* This may be even more important in a virtual environment—give first and often.

► Be *courteous.* Just because a message is online doesn't mean real-world conventions don't apply. Use salutations ("Dear [name]") and complimentary closings ("Best regards," "Sincerely," etc.). Pay attention to grammar and spelling.

► Do *be respectful of other people's time.* Even an e-mail has a time cost.

Virtual Networking Don'ts

► Don't *give out other people's e-mail addresses.* They're just as personal as phone numbers or addresses.

► *Don't give out e-mail introductions carelessly.* If you have any doubt, be sure to check with the person who is the target of the referral.

► *Don't post anything online you wouldn't want to see published in the newspaper or discussed on CNN.* Once you post information online, you can't take it back. Even if you delete the information from a site, older versions may exist on other people's computers. The same applies to e-mail.

► *Don't be verbose.* You're not writing an essay.

► *Don't be aggressive or hostile in any way.* You'll get a reputation.

We've Only Just Begun

Virtual networking has been around a lot longer than MySpace and LinkedIn. Online social networking as we know it today came about as a sort of compilation of previous forms of online and virtual communication developed to accommodate continually changing social needs. It is far from a fad; it is an evolution still in progress.

Despite the publicity surrounding the popular social networking sites, we should realize that similar, less-heralded systems have proven successful within organizations as well. Accessibility to information in general, and in particular to human capital/experience, can be invaluable for an organization. Scaling up the potential of interpersonal contact in any scenario is ideal for all involved, and even personal networking has become more common as a result of the prominence of online social networking.

While you need to be careful in how you network online, the fact remains that linking people to one another is a brilliant concept, no matter how you look at it. Being able to read about and come into contact with people from other regions or countries can abolish a lot of barriers (such as stereotypes, for example). The world is globalizing, and distance is no longer the same factor it was in making and maintaining contact with others even a decade ago. However, it is difficult to imagine that only one-sixth of the world's population has access to the Internet and yet that has changed the way the world works. Just think of the kind of world we will live in when half, even one-quarter, of the world has the benefits of exposure that come from the Internet. It should not surprise anyone that oppressive regimes limit or restrict people's Internet access. Information, personal contact, and outside perspectives are such powerful tools, and it is incredible to see how the world continues to change as more and more people realize this power and become a part of online social networking.

In the next chapter we'll peer into the crystal ball in an attempt to catch a glimpse of the future of networking.

Conclusion

The Future of Networking

I said at the outset of this book that networking is about more than the number of business cards you hand out, the size of your Rolodex, or the amount of phone numbers stored in your BlackBerry: it can be a way of life. I hope that you now see how true that statement is. The Connect Effect can be a powerful force in our personal lives, in our organizations, and in society at large. But what does the future hold for the Connect Effect?

With globalization, new communication technologies, and changing demographics, to cite only a few factors, society is changing at a rapid pace—as is the world of work and organizations. What will networking look like in the future? I don't have a crystal ball and don't claim that I can accurately predict the future, but I do have some ideas on the future of networking—and of the issues we will be grappling with over the next few years.

As I noted in the preface, I interviewed more than thirty people from all walks of life for this book. You've already met many of them. At the end of each interview I asked this question: "Can you speculate on the future of networking?" I received some very thoughtful comments, as people raised a number of issues that they thought would be of increasing importance in the years ahead. In broad terms, the issues raised dealt with how networking is affecting careers and organizations, with our conceptions of community and society, with the impact of the Internet and new communications technology, and with the continued importance of the personal touch despite all that technology.

Below are excerpts from the interviews that address each of these four areas. At the end of the chapter, I will offer my own predictions.

Careers and Organizations

The world of work is changing. Do current trends make networking an increasingly important tool for managing your career and understanding organizations? Or will technology replace networking as a tool? The people I talked with suggest that networking will only grow in importance.

Vince Perro, Former President, Leadership Consulting,
Heidrick & Struggles

I would say that networking is increasingly a fact of life and an understanding that is, in essence, almost built in for the newer generations of people in business. I think—and that's driven by a number of things—that the biggest will be the change in the employer-employee relationship. For a lot of us, in our professional cohort, when we were starting out in business, there was still a predominance of executive employees who basically went to one company and stayed there for a long time. And so the networks—particularly external networks—really weren't as important as they are today.

But today, the employment relationship is a lot different. It is more of a temporal relationship. Companies and individuals come together for periods of time when there's a mutuality of interest, but the employee doesn't make a long-term commitment to the company and the company doesn't make a long-term commitment to the employee in the way that they used to. And that means that networks for individuals are much more important than they used to be.

And frankly, they're important both internally and externally in this fluid, just-in-time talent or staffing kind of environment in which we live. There need to be more efficient ways of connecting people with the roles they need to be in. For this purpose, companies almost need their own networks. Individuals need to do their networks internally as well as externally in order to connect with the right opportunities that make the best use of their skills.

So I think it's become increasingly important for those reasons. I think you will see it more and more bred into the newer generations who have grown up in this environment.

Rob Cross, Associate Professor in the Management Department, University of Virginia's McIntire School of Commerce, and Author of The Hidden Power of Social Networks

My work tends to be built much more around understanding face-to-face collaborations in organizations. So I can't necessarily speak to the Friendsters or LinkedIns as a broad networking technology. But what does hold a lot of promise is the knowledge-network system at companies like Microsoft because they're showing relationships and making them visible.

I think the basic problem that systems like Friendster and LinkedIn are always going to run up against is time—people's time and willingness to respond. How do you better solve a real challenge just because people can get to me and figure out who I know? This doesn't mean that I'm going to help them get connected. I think that the challenge of time isn't going to be overcome with more technology.

Secondly, I hope to see networking systems move toward something at an individual level, somewhat like these personal network profiles. What I believe people probably need is some sort of ability to visualize how and where they're spending their time relationally and to continually refine their own connectivity in ways that make them more productive. As I was saying earlier on, as collaborations become more central to pretty much everything, dynamically visualizing and analyzing one's network is the kind of thing that could probably result in freeing up people's time so they can invest it more productively.

Marshall Goldsmith, Executive Coach and Author of
What Got You Here Won't Get You There

I think it's going to become more and more important because as you look forward—again, as Peter Drucker said, "The leader of the past knew how to tell; the leader of the future knows how to ask." More and more when you manage knowledge workers, you're not managing idiots. You're managing very bright people, and what you need to do is build network relationships with them. You don't treat them like subordinates; you treat them like colleagues. So I think the distinction between "I'm your boss" and "I'm your peer" will start blurring. More and more people are going to focus on being partners and helping each other.

John Zapolski, Partner, Management Innovation Group

I think technology innovations will continue to impact networking, both in the social sphere as well as in the professional sphere. I think a lot of these social networking technologies are going to be adapted for the business community. Especially as younger generations enter the workforce, organizations will be forced to integrate these technologies into the fabric of the operations.

Without a doubt, the future's going to be much more highly networked, much more facilitated by technology, much more driven by small-scale interactions, and much more organized by informal kinds of networks than we've seen in the past. So in other words, we'll see many fewer business professional organizations that have conferences and annual meetings and much more collaboration by people through wikis and other forms of online collaboration.

New technology modes that haven't even been invented yet will continue the trend of finding people who you'll benefit from knowing or benefit from working with and facilitating all that online. At the same time, I don't think face-to-face networking goes away. I think face-to-face continues to be very important in that there's a certain kind of interaction you can have with people when you're present in the same room with them that you'll just never be able to do exclusively through technology. But I think that technology connections—the connections that you build and maintain at a distance through technology—will just be used to facilitate face-to-face meetings.

Jim Kouzes, Coauthor of The Leadership Challenge

If my own personal experience and research is any indication, what we will see is more extensive use of both the face-to-face interpersonal as well as the networks that are facilitated by technology. And we'll see those expand beyond the borders of our office or our industry or our country to truly global networks. So we'll be able to talk to people in other countries.

I'll tell you another funny six-degrees-of-separation story that highlights just how connected we all are. When I was a sophomore in high school in 1961, we brought an exchange student here to this country to live with us. We sponsored him as a family. Fast forward to 1989, so almost thirty years later, and Otto Vockary, who lived in our house in 1961–62, translated *The Leadership Challenge* into Finnish.

It's that kind of global connection that once you make it, and if it's the kind that builds and develops over a period of time, you'll see, in very strange and unusual ways, reappear down the road. It may be thirty years into the future. So I think it's really important that we do pay close attention to networking. It's not just another fad. It is a fact.

The other thing that I think will happen, however, is that as MySpace, YouTube, and the electronic networks mature, people will realize their limitations. People will realize that they're not a substitute for the real thing. There is a difference between a flesh-and-blood connection with somebody and what you can do electronically. People will realize that there are just some things you cannot do virtually.

In terms of leadership, for instance, we know from our research that a person's most immediate supervisor is the most important manager in your organization. It is not the CEO. It is not even your manager's manager. It is your immediate supervisor. So globally, while networks may be useful in terms of coordination, collaboration, sharing of information, sharing of ideas, even developing new ideas, they have their limitations when it comes to managing.

I would suggest that one of the things we'll learn is that we need to find a way to utilize the most direct contact we have for the more day-to-day feeding and managing of an organization. And that leadership over distances, if you will, will be of a different nature—probably more in the way of thought leadership or more strategic, but not necessarily operational.

Community and Society

Rapid change creates stress in the fabric of our communities and in society as old roles, structures, and relationships give way to new ones. Networking seems to be a powerful force for coping with social change—even an essential "survival strategy," according to one interviewee.

Tammy Erickson, President, The Concours Institute,
BSG Concours

I think what we're going to see going forward is that the concept of networking will, in many ways, merge with the concept of democracy, or choice. So, in other words, as we are more able to interact with our environment, whether it's our work environment or political environment or whatever, individual voices will become more prominent because we have the electronic communication means to do so. Networking will focus on areas or places where we want to make an impact—places where we want to connect and create value, create revenue, and so on.

I see networking not so much as "I want to know you or have you do something for me" but because I want to plug into you and either express my view or hook up with you to create value. This will be more the concept behind networks going forward. This is much deeper than the almost frivolous connotation networking can have in some ways.

The value of being connected will become much more pronounced around issues of mass creation and cocreation and coinfluence and democracy instead of around who do I feel good about and who can I chat with. It's going to have a real value creation feel to it. So it's a critically important topic to master going forward.

Peter Sims, Coauthor of True North: Discover Your Authentic Leadership

I'll take a very macroperspective first. If you look at the research that exists on community and on networks that exist in the United States, it's very clear that those types of connections have dwindled over time. Especially the in-person connections have dwindled over time. If you look at what Robert Putnam wrote in *Bowling Alone*, it becomes very clear what the patterns are.

So one has to ask, "What's the response to that? How do people within their communities, or within their organizations or companies, respond to the need to be around people?" Because it's also very clear that human beings have a need to be associated with other people.

I think you can see a response to this dichotomy in terms of the evangelical church movement in this country, where people like Rick Warren have built churches within a church (six-person groups within a very large church) to give people the chance to have intimate connections and bonds with others. And this has been an enormously successful mechanism to drive the growth of this evangelical church movement.

Malcolm Gladwell has written about this, and I think the same needs that these evangelical churches are tapping into apply to those who work in companies. For example, I've even heard of companies offering services—consulting services to corporations—to facilitate groups of six to eight people that would meet for very open discussions about what's important to them so that better team dynamics can be established. I think that trend is going to continue, even though there's always a tension in the corporate world between having open and, dare we say, intimate conversations within an organization and what it takes to make a productive team—what it takes to be running on all cylinders.

I come at these issues in terms of the in-person dynamic because I don't think, even with all that's been written and said about the technology tools, that these virtual interactions can completely supplant interaction in person. It has to be a combination of the two approaches. Companies are going to have to find ways to allow people to communicate more easily, but they also have to take that a step further to find ways to allow people to have those in-person interactions from which they can advance their own development and also feel bound to the culture and goals of the organization.

John Foster, Head of Talent Management and Organization Development at IDEO

I'll go back to Alvin Toffler in *Future Shock* and say that we're just living out what he said would happen. The three things I pull out of that are learn to learn, learn to choose, and learn to relate: these are his three critical competencies necessary to succeed in the future. I believe the future is now, and those are the three core competencies people need to have to function.

Robert Wright, in his book *Nonzero*, says that the destiny of human beings is to get more complex, that it's our genetic predisposition to create complexity. I think that networking is becoming more and more important as a way to navigate an increasingly complex world. *The World Is Flat* [by Thomas Friedman] is another really good book that characterizes a future with fewer artificial barriers and boundaries, thus creating many more opportunities to connect. Networking, then, becomes more and more prevalent. Networking is becoming more of the de facto survival strategy.

Technology and the Internet

New technology is bringing instant access to information, ideas, and people. The consensus is that technology will only accelerate our ability to network.

Barbara Howes, Vice President, Disney University,
The Walt Disney Company

Virtual networking finally has the right tools in everybody's hands. You almost have no excuse not to network. You can blog, interact in a chat room, connect via e-mail to anybody, anywhere, anytime. Here at Disney, we're looking for ways that we can enable networks with the right technology, the right funding, but also the right support. There's tremendous collaboration that can come out of a network. Networks are where we learn what our next lines of business will be.

Tony DiRomualdo, Founder, Next Generation Workplace

Networking is being made easier because of the technology. It's a lot easier to stay in touch with people or to reach out to people because of these various capabilities. For example, on the Internet, things like LinkedIn allow you to share your contact information with another person's network. So networks are actually being made explicit, and there are more explicit ways to get introduced and get plugged into networks.

When we look at people with blogs and/or profiles on MySpace—whether it's their thoughts, work, comments about things that are really interesting to them—it's very easy now for those who are looking for like-minded people to connect and network. I think that capability is going to continue to grow. It's amazing when we look at something like MySpace or Facebook that they went from zero users to tens of millions of users in less than two years.

I think networking is becoming even more important in business today. Businesses are so dynamic, so volatile, and careers have become so dynamic that people really have to rely more than ever on building and connecting into really solid, deep networks of people who they can jointly work with; have as sources of information, guidance, and knowledge; and even help with getting a job. I think we'll see more virtualization of business with an emphasis on collaboration.

The challenge is that getting skilled at networking is not something that is easily taught. It's not like you can take a networking course. Some people have a natural networking ability. But I think having some pragmatic guidance to help people think through how they can be much more effective networkers is critical to anybody, no matter what generation you happen to be in.

Teddy Zmrhal, Partner, Congruity

I think we'll see a lot more visualization—the ability to visualize this reflection and feedback. Sites like Digg and even Spoke have this cool ability to look at the way you connect with other people. But it's still in its infancy. Getting feedback on how many people you interact with and how often, with little reminders—that would be very useful.

I have my Outlook set up to prompt me when it's the birthday of people in my network. So then they come up at least once a year. For people I haven't talked to in a while, I get to say, "Hey, happy birthday. What's going on?" I also think we'll see more awareness of what it means to be in a network and how that really works.

Patricia Franklin, Chief Learning Officer,
Vistage International, Inc.

I think LinkedIn has demonstrated to us that networking can happen even with perfect strangers. If you are also talking to any self-respecting gamer going into a massively multiplayer online game, a genre that I'm familiar with (and that's been alive and kicking for several decades), you can easily connect with people now, electronically, in a very meaningful way. I've had astonishing experiences on LinkedIn by being able to just get to people within organizations that otherwise probably wouldn't even pick up the phone. I really see LinkedIn merging with things like Second Life.

The Personal Touch

The Internet is a wonderful tool—but will it replace the personal touch? Our need for intimate contact with others will not go away. Technology may even make personal, face-to-face connections more important than ever, according to many of the people I spoke with.

Bill Morin, Career Management Expert, Author, and
Founder and Former Chairman of Drake Beam Morin, Inc.

I think there's going to be a return to the human element. Today, we're so networked online and through television and mass media that we feel almost overwhelmed that way, and we yearn for the human touch. Which of us doesn't want to have someone that's a human being listening to us? Even if we're trying to do it through the mass media.

I think it's always going to be true that we will need to have personal and professional contacts, but I think it will become even more critical in the future. In almost every case, the first five minutes of talk need to be spent on trying to build a connection between you and the contact. "Where are you from? Where have you worked? Whom do you know there?" I think that's an indication of how important networking is because we're trying to figure out, Where the heck do we fit in the middle of that person's network? Can we get in it? In that first five minutes of a conversation, you're making decisions. Do you trust the individual? Do you respect the individual? Do you think the person can have any possible impact on your career and your life? Do you find them intelligent? Some major decisions are made very quickly.

Al Samuels, Improvisational Comedian and Star of the NBC Sitcom Sports Action Team

I believe my network will reach all around the world. But ironically, I will feel less connected unless I am careful to stay connected to my neighbor, my best friend from high school, and the people that I like to hang with and go out with on a Friday night. Because now it's just as easy, if not easier, to talk to somebody in India on MySpace or via e-mail than it is to go down the street and see my dear friend of the last twenty years.

Networking will become more global in nature, but I think at the same time, people will feel the need to continue or go back to more human interaction, where it's not just via e-mail, a cell phone, or IM.

Richard Leider, Executive Coach and Author of Repacking Your Bags *and* Claiming Your Place at the Fire: Living the Second Half of Your Life on Purpose

What I'm observing is that a lot of leaders and managers and professionals mistake this 24/7 technology—this high-tech world—for communications, for real touch with people. There was a brilliant article by Edwin Hallowell in the *Harvard Business Review*, I think, a year or two ago. It was called "The Human Moment at Work." I think what's really missing increasingly with speed, technology, globalization, etc., is the human moment.

A lot of times we mistake technologies—like conference calls, like meetings where we're not together—for real communication or real networking. So I think with all this technology, my speculation is that there's going to be more meetings, not less. And those meetings are going to need to be increasingly high-tech. Not just in the bar or the hallway or at dinners or luncheons.

But we're really going to have to share stories and get to know each other culturally and cross-culturally and network with each other in much more depth for organization cultures to survive in a healthy way in the future. So I predict more meetings, not less, based on the technology. I'm finding that once we go to an offsite, all I have to do is get out of the way because people are just dying to talk with each other.

My Take on the Future

As you can see, there is some general agreement on the future of networking. We'll see more and better technology-enabled tools. (But even with all of the new bells and whistles, networking is still something that you need to take time to plan, execute, and build into your daily life.) Networking will continue to be an important part of organizational life. We'll see a return to and reemphasis on the human element in networking. The younger generations are and will be much better at networking than the plus-forty crowd ever was (or will be). Now I am going to step out on a limb and make my own predictions.

Put the Connect Effect to Work for You

The power of networking, what I have been calling the "Connect Effect," is undeniable. Throughout history, networks have changed the world. What was the Underground Railroad but a

Top Ten Networking Predictions

1. It'll be much easier to build, maintain, and leverage our networks. New tools and capabilities will emerge that will improve the efficiency and effectiveness of our networking activities. We'll see "network agents" (like Visible Path) that will mine our e-mail, phone calls, and documents and automatically help us make connections. We'll see systems that will prompt us, saying, for example, that it's time to network with so-and-so because we have not been in touch for six months. We'll be able to graph or visualize our networks to help us better understand their strengths and weaknesses.

2. Networks will expand globally. Automated translation programs will help enable this expansion.

3. We'll be able to have much better visual connectivity with our network members. We'll feel like we're face-to-face, though we actually won't be. I'm not talking about virtual reality networking per se, but at a minimum, we'll be sending each other personal video clips, not text e-mails.

4. We'll leverage the Global Positioning System (GPS) to connect with people who are in close physical proximity to us. Massachusetts Institute of Technology's Media Lab has already created a system that can send you a text message when someone it determines you should meet (via a profile database) is in close proximity to you (you and this person are tracked by GPS). Or imagine how great it would be to know that someone in your network is at O'Hare Airport at the same time you are waiting for a plane. You might be able to meet and have a drink together.

►

5. We'll begin to see businesses that aren't simply mail-list providers but network service providers (NSPs). These companies will specialize in creating connections between people on a massive scale. They'll not simply know someone's name, position, and address; they'll have a wealth of information that can be used to connect people with each other. In a sense, an NSP will be a "networking concierge service" that deeply understands your needs and helps you meet the right people. NSPs will also keep you updated on people within your network (like a news clipping service) and help you effectively maintain your network.

6. Networks will form to more closely connect gurus (people with wisdom) to practitioners. The practitioners will form networks or communities to discuss the guru's wisdom and apply it in a practical manner in their own lives or work context. Lessons learned will be shared among the network members (and the gurus themselves).

7. A networking metalanguage or set of standards will emerge so that all of our networking devices and software are interoperable.

8. While all of the technology-enabled networking capabilities and tools will produce many benefits, in parallel we'll see a return to more personal networking via face-to-face or synchronous connections because certain types of connections can only be established face-to-face.

9. A U.S. presidential candidate will be elected largely based upon his or her ability to leverage the Connect Effect.

10. *The Connect Effect* will become an international bestseller, the author will appear on *Oprah* and the *Today* show, a movie will be produced, and the author will retire to the Caribbean to network with fish. (Just kidding!)

network of people who helped free thousands of slaves before the Civil War? During World War II, networks of resistance fighters in France battled the Nazis. Two thousand years ago, Christianity was spread throughout the Roman world by a network of proselytizers—profoundly changing the course of history. If you want to change the world, or just your life, you can do it with a network. I hope that this book has given you the information you need to transform your personal and professional networks.

I urge you to reassess your NQ a few months after reading this book, after you have had a chance to put into effect some of the lessons you've learned. I have reproduced the questionnaire from chapter 1 below. If you practice what you have learned in this book, your NQ should go up considerably. You will be on your way to the Network Zone, where all things are possible because you know the right people to make them happen.

And again, I invite you to meet me virtually at my Web site, http://www.theconnecteffect.com, to keep up on the latest concerning the Connect Effect.

Determining Your New NQ

Two components go into your NQ: part A focuses on the scope and strength of your existing network, and part B focuses on how active you are in building and maintaining your network. With these components in mind, assess your NQ by honestly answering the following questions on a scale of 0–4:

Part A: Network Scope and Strength

1. How many total people are in your personal, professional, and virtual networks? Add them all together.

   0 = Under 10

   1 = 11–100

   2 = 101–200

   3 = 201–400

   4 = more than 400

2. How strong are your relationships with the people in your network? Are the people in your network just *business-card traders* (you traded cards but can hardly remember where or when), *acquaintances* (they know who you are and will probably return a call), *personal contacts* (they'll do a favor if you ask), or *close friends* (you can count on them when the chips are down)?

   0 = All business

   1 = Mostly acquaintances

   2 = Lots of personal contacts

   3 = A mix of personal contacts and close friends

   4 = Mostly close friends with a few personal contacts and acquaintances

3. How diverse is your network? If everyone you know is the same age and sex as you, shares your cultural background, and works in the same area, your network is not diverse at all. On the other hand, if you network with people from eight to eighty, of both sexes, with a variety of cultural backgrounds, and in different kinds of jobs in different industries, you have a very diverse network.

   0 = Looking at my network is like looking in a mirror.

   1 = My network includes mostly people like me, but it has some diversity.

   2 = My network has a good amount of diversity.

   3 = My network includes people from a wide variety of backgrounds and industries.

4 = My network includes many people from a wide variety of backgrounds, interests, and industries.

4. What's the overall quality of your network contacts? Are the people in your network experienced, with significant accomplishments? Do they have strong networks of their own? Are they well known within a professional sphere? Can they open doors for you?

0 = I like them, but they aren't movers and shakers by any means.

1 = A few people have some connections.

2 = Some people in my network really command attention.

3 = Many people in my network are at the top of their fields and very well connected.

4 = I can contact almost anyone on earth through the people in my network.

Part B: Networking Activities

5. To what extent do you actively work on building your network relationships? Do you follow up after the first meeting? Do you make sure to periodically connect with people? Do you return phone calls and answer e-mails promptly? Do you try to meet face-to-face regularly?

0 = I don't have time for all that.

1 = I try to reach out if I can find the time.

2 = I try to make time, but it's hit or miss.

3 = I consistently make time to connect with people.

4 = I make connecting with people my top priority every day.

6. How often do you actively recruit new members to your network?

0 = Never

1 = Rarely

2 = Sometimes

3 = Often

4 = All the time

7. How often do you help others in your network (both when asked for help and unsolicited)?

0 = Never
1 = Rarely
2 = Sometimes
3 = Often
4 = All the time

8. To what extent do you leverage the Internet to build and maintain your networks?

0 = Never
1 = Rarely
2 = Sometimes
3 = Often
4 = All the time

Add your scores together and multiply the total by 5. You'll end up with an NQ between 0 and 160. The following chart interprets your score:

0–80 **Below Average**—networking has not been on your radar screen
You need to be much more active in establishing and maintaining connections.

81–110 **Average**—nothing to brag about
You could benefit from being much more proactive.

111–140 **Above Average**—a natural networker
You are doing well, but a more systematic effort can help.

141–160 **Networking Genius!**
You know it takes ongoing effort to maintain your network.

Resource A

Choosing Your Board

Finding Support for Making Sound Choices

by Richard Leider
(http://www.inventuregroup.com)

t is essential to know yourself. Once you have gone through a process to create self-awareness, you are ready to choose the right people to sit on your board to help you make sound choices. Who do you want on your board and why do you want them? Just as important, what do you expect from them and what do you have to offer them?

Why Do You Want Them?

We assume you want board members who have wisdom. By this we mean people who understand the importance of heeding your life's calling and living and working on purpose.

Naming your purpose is the first step in your quest to working and living on purpose. In answering the question, "Who are you?" many questions usually come up. They may include:

- What does working and living on purpose look like?

- What does succeeding look like at this stage of your life?

- How do you envision the hoped-for future and how do you get there?

► How do you hold yourself accountable for the goals you have set?

These are the kinds of questions your Sounding Board can help you to answer.

Selecting Your Sounding Board

Your Sounding Board is made up of trusted individuals who listen well and offer you courageous conversation. They may have only one thing in common—you! But they all meet the following criteria:

They're interested (versus interesting)
They are genuinely interested in you and want to see you succeed.

They care (versus cure)
They are not interested in fixing you, but care about you as you are.

They listen deeply
They are focused on listening to you and are not distracted by other concerns or issues when they are with you.

They ask great questions
They don't seek to tell you what you need, but ask questions to help you discover the answers within yourself.

They practice courageous conversation
They are honest with you and will tell you the truth.

Your Sounding Board can include your spouse/partner, family members, colleagues, models and mentors, friends, coaches, teachers, spiritual advisors, and wise elders. If you convened your board to discuss a major life/work challenge or your future direction, who would be sitting around the table with you? If you don't relate to a board table, consider a circle, a campfire, or a coffee table.

My Sounding Board

To begin selecting board members, list below those people who you typically call when you need someone to listen to you, guide you, or tell you the truth.

1. Friends or relatives I can call or visit when I need to make a sound choice.

2. Mentors or guides who can serve as sounding boards for my choices and actions.

3. Professional friends and resources who are available to me as part of a sounding board (i.e., colleagues, financial planning counselors).

4. Spiritual and community advisors (e.g., community leaders, clergypersons) that can offer me support in challenging times.

5. Wise elders and teachers who help me see the big picture.

Sounding Board Selection Checklist

It's time to select your Sounding Board: three to five individuals who will serve as your Sounding Board for one year. The following questions are designed for you to ask yourself about a potential board member. The more insight you have about a person and his or her attitudes, philosophies, hopes, and values, the more clearly you can work together. The more ways in which you are connected to a board member, the more you are going to trust that person enough to reveal yourself to him or her.

These five questions do not constitute a quiz that one can pass or fail, but they will give you some awareness of key criteria for effective board members.

*What is the single most important **quality** this person has added to my life?*

*If you had a serious **challenge**, how do you think this person would respond?*

*Can you think of a time when this person **listened deeply** to you?*

Does this person reflect more or less than you do? Can you name a book you think you would both enjoy reading?

Can you think of a time when you had a courageous conversation (deep truth telling) with this person?

Other Sounding Board Members

When creating your Sounding Board, don't be afraid to make an unconventional selection. Choose your favorite author, a biblical or historical figure, someone you knew who has passed on, or a fictional character from a book or movie to serve on your board. Imagine what these people would tell you if you could talk with them. Consider what you know about them and apply their wisdom to your situation.

Sarah is a professional in the insurance industry. Early in her career, Sarah relied on a mentor to help her when she faced challenges in her professional and, sometimes, her personal life. Although this mentor passed away a few years ago, Sarah still "consults" with him when she faces difficult decisions or challenges in her life. She imagines how her mentor might have responded if they could converse, and she takes his advice to heart.

Sounding Board Selection Checklist

To help you narrow down your board to three to five members, put a check next to each person's name who meets the criteria suggested in each of the five board selection questions.

Names of Potential Board Members	1. Adds Quality	2. Responds to Challenges	3. Listens Deeply	4. Reflects	5. Holds Courageous Conversations
Friends or Relatives: _____ _____ _____					
Mentors or Guides: _____ _____ _____					

Professional Friends or Resources: ___ ___ ___ ▲ ▲ ▲				
Spiritual and Community Groups: ___ ___ ___ ▲ ▲ ▲				
Wise Elders and Teachers: ___ ___ ___ ▲ ▲ ▲				

Resource B

Online Networking Sites

New networking sites are being born every day. Rather than create a list here on paper that will be instantly outdated, I am going to list a few sites you can check out online that can get you started exploring the Internet for networking opportunities. You should also check out my own Web site, which will be updated regularly with networking links: http://www.theconnecteffect.com.

An eclectic mix of online communities, chat rooms, and message boards can be found at the following site:

- ► http://dmoz.org/Computers/Internet/Cyberspace/Online _Communities/

The following sites provide listings of social networking sites (with some overlap):

- ► http://www.rateitall.com/t-1900-social-networking- web-sites.aspx

- ► http://www.rev2.org/2006/07/11/33-places-to-hangout-in- the-social-networking-era/

Wikipedia provides a large list of social and professional networking sites here:

► http://en.wikipedia.org/wiki/List_of_social _networking_websites

If you like social action—the environment, women's issues, human rights, animal activism, and more—check out these two sites:

► http://www.care2.com

► http://www.change.org.

Professional/business oriented networking sites include the following:

► www.fastpitchnetworking.com/

► www.linkedin.com

► www.tribe.net

► www.ryze.com

These are just a few ideas to get you started. You can also search for "social networks," "business networks," and similar terms on your favorite Internet search engine.

Notes

1. Nobelprize.org, "The Nobel Peace Prize 2006," http:// nobelprize.org/nobel_prizes/peace/laureates/2006/.
2. Tim Sanders, "Love Is the Killer App," *Fast Company*, January 2002, 64.
3. R. Cross, T. Davenport, and S. Cantrell, "The Social Side of High Performance," *Sloan Management Review* 45, no. 1 (2003): 20–24.
4. Jim Bolt, "The Power of Peer-to-Peer Networks," FastCompany.com, November 14, 2005, http://www .fastcompany.com/resources/learning/conner/111405 .html.
5. Richard O'Leary, telephone interview by author, February 14, 2007.
6. Deborah Swanson, telephone interview by author, February 20, 2007.
7. Chuck Presbury, telephone interview by author, February 22, 2007.
8. Lev Grossman, "Time's Person of the Year: You," *Time*, December 13, 2006, http://www.time.com/time/magazine/ article/0,9171,1569514,00.html.

Index

Acknowledgments

First of all, I'd like to thank my wife, Teresa, and son, Theo, for putting up with me while I wrote this book. You are my greatest source of happiness, and I love you with all my heart. Next, I'd like to thank all of the staff at Berrett-Koehler. Publishing with you has been a joy, and I appreciate the attention and care you've shown me and this book. A special thank-you goes to Johanna Vondeling for believing in this book from the start and expertly shepherding it from inception to completion. I'd also like to thank Jeevan Sivasubramaniam for making the book publishing process fun (or as fun as it can possibly be!).

I'd like to thank all of the people that I interviewed and those who contributed to this book. Your insights, experience, and wisdom made this book come alive. They include Etienne Wenger, Marshall Goldsmith, Richard Leider, Bill Morin, Teddy Zmrhal, Nisha Advani, Rick Smith, Peter Sims, Patricia Franklin, Lynda Gratton, Jim Kouzes, Vince Perro, Jeff Rosenthal, Tammy Erickson, Jory Des Jardins, Jack Dulworth, Rob Cross, Scott Saslow, Dan Morrison, Kristen Kemerling, John Zapolski, Scott Hirsch, Steve Graubart, Michael Drapkin, JoAnne Black, Tony DiRomualdo, Barbara Howes, Al Samuels,

John Foster, Antony Brydon, Kathleen Bruno, and Harvey Singh.

I'd like to acknowledge and thank all of the staff (full-time and contractual) of Executive Networks, my board of directors, and our wonderful clients. So much of what I know about networks and networking I've learned from you. My *awesome* interns from the summer of 2006, Alexander Neagoe from the University of Michigan and Joel Curado Silveirinha from the University of Portugal, deserve a lot of credit for helping me conduct research for the book, especially on virtual and social networks. One of my best friends, Lisa Gesner, is a wonderful editor and helped to make my writing appear much better than it was in the book's first draft. Sam Case helped me rewrite and reorganize the second draft of the book, and I'd like to thank him for this assistance.

I'd like to provide a special thank-you to Alan Shrader. Alan, an extraordinary writer and developmental editor, has fundamentally become my coauthor. He worked tirelessly to help me create the third (and final!) draft of the book, and most of the credit goes to him for making the book readable and cogent.

And lastly, I'd like to send a heartfelt thank-you to Jim Bolt, who believed in me and my vision enough in 2003 to sell me the company (Executive Development Associates, Inc.) that he'd spent the previous twenty years building into such a powerful and well-respected brand. You've been the best partner, mentor, coach, and friend I could ever have imagined, and you are truly an Obi-Wan Kenobi.

About the Author

Michael Dulworth is the chairman and CEO of Executive Networks, Inc. Executive Networks is a leading provider of executive peer-to-peer networks to large organizations worldwide (http://www.executivenetworks.com). Prior to his current position, Mike was vice president of learning services at the Concours Group and was a founder and CEO of Learning Technologies Group, Inc. Mike is the author, a coauthor, or a contributor to six books on executive development, learning, and high-performance organizations. His most recent books are *Corporate Learning: Proven and Practical Guidelines for Building a Sustainable Learning Strategy* (Pfeiffer, 2005) and *Strategic Executive Development: The Five Essential Investments* (Pfeiffer, 2005). Mike has a bachelor of arts degree from the University of Michigan and a masters in public administration, with a concentration in organizational behavior, from the University of Southern California.

About Berrett-Koehler Publishers

Berrett-Koehler is an independent publisher dedicated to an ambitious mission: **Creating a World That Works for All.**

We believe that to truly create a better world, action is needed at all levels—individual, organizational, and societal. At the individual level, our publications help people align their lives with their values and with their aspirations for a better world. At the organizational level, our publications promote progressive leadership and management practices, socially responsible approaches to business, and humane and effective organizations. At the societal level, our publications advance social and economic justice, shared prosperity, sustainability, and new solutions to national and global issues.

A major theme of our publications is "Opening Up New Space." They challenge conventional thinking, introduce new ideas, and foster positive change. Their common quest is changing the underlying beliefs, mindsets, institutions, and structures that keep generating the same cycles of problems, no matter who our leaders are or what improvement programs we adopt.

We strive to practice what we preach—to operate our publishing company in line with the ideas in our books. At the core of our approach is stewardship, which we define as a deep sense of responsibility to administer the company for the benefit of all of our "stakeholder" groups: authors, customers, employees, investors, service providers, and the communities and environment around us.

We are grateful to the thousands of readers, authors, and other friends of the company who consider themselves to be part of the "BK Community." We hope that you, too, will join us in our mission.

Be Connected

Visit Our Website

Go to www.bkconnection.com to read exclusive previews and excerpts of new books, find detailed information on all Berrett-Koehler titles and authors, browse subject-area libraries of books, and get special discounts.

Subscribe to Our Free E-Newsletter

Be the first to hear about new publications, special discount offers, exclusive articles, news about bestsellers, and more! Get on the list for our free e-newsletter by going to www.bkconnection.com.

Get Quantity Discounts

Berrett-Koehler books are available at quantity discounts for orders of ten or more copies. Please call us toll-free at (800) 929-2929 or email us at bkp.orders@aidcvt.com.

Host a Reading Group

For tips on how to form and carry on a book reading group in your workplace or community, see our website at www.bkconnection.com.

Join the BK Community

Thousands of readers of our books have become part of the "BK Community" by participating in events featuring our authors, reviewing draft manuscripts of forthcoming books, spreading the word about their favorite books, and supporting our publishing program in other ways. If you would like to join the BK Community, please contact us at bkcommunity@bkpub.com.